Date Due

OP 14   3X 06 (90)

The Archbishop's Ceiling

The American Clock

BY ARTHUR MILLER

PLAYS

All My Sons
Death of a Salesman
An Enemy of the People (*adaptation*)
The Crucible
A Memory of Two Mondays
A View from the Bridge
After the Fall
Incident at Vichy
The Price
The Creation of the World and Other Business
The Archbishop's Ceiling
The American Clock
Two-way Mirror
Danger: Memory!

SCREENPLAYS

The Misfits
Playing for Time
Almost Everybody Wins

FICTION

Focus (*novel*)
I Don't Need You Any More (*stories*)
Jane's Blanket (*for children*)

NONFICTION

Situation Normal
"Salesman" in Beijing
Timebends: A Life

WITH INGE MORATH

In Russia
In the Country
Chinese Encounters

COLLECTIONS

Arthur Miller's Collected Plays
The Portable Arthur Miller
The Theater Essays of Arthur Miller

ARTHUR MILLER

The Archbishop's Ceiling

The American Clock

TWO PLAYS

with an introduction by the author

GROVE PRESS
New York

Published by Grove Press, a division of Wheatland Corporation
841 Broadway, New York, N.Y. 10003

CAUTION: Professionals and amateurs are hereby warned that *The Archbishop's Ceiling* and *The American Clock,* being fully protected under the Copyright Laws of the United States of America, the British Commonwealth, including the Dominion of Canada, and all other countries of the Berne and Universal Copyright Conventions, are subject to royalty. All rights, including professional, amateur, motion picture, recitation, lecturing, public reading, and radio and television broadcasting, and the rights of translation into foreign languages, are strictly reserved. Particular emphasis is laid on the question of readings, permission for which must be secured in writing from the author's agent, International Creative Management, Inc., 40 West 57th Street, New York, N.Y. 10019.

Library of Congress Cataloging-in-Publication Data

Miller, Arthur, 1915–
[Archbishop's ceiling]
The Archbishop's ceiling; and, The American clock: two plays/
Arthur Miller, with an introduction by the author.—1st ed.
p.   cm.
ISBN 0-8021-1085-1.   ISBN 0-8021-3127-1 (pbk.)
I. Miller, Arthur, 1915–   American clock. 1988. II. Title.
PS3525.I5156A88 1988   88-19155
812'.52—dc19   CIP

Designed by Irving Perkins Associates
Manufactured in the United States of America
This book is printed on acid-free paper.
First Edition 1989
10   9   8   7   6   5   4   3   2   1

CONTENTS

INTRODUCTION

Conditions of Freedom:

Two Plays of the Seventies

I

It is pointless any longer to speak of a period as being one of transition—what period isn't?—but the seventies, when both these plays were written, seemed to resist any definition even at the time. *The Archbishop's Ceiling* in some part was a response to this indefinition I sensed around me. Early in the decade the Kent State massacre took place, and while the anti–Vietnam War movement could still mobilize tens of thousands, the freshness had gone out of the wonderful sixties mixture of idealism and bitterness that had sought to project a new unaggressive society based on human connection rather than the values of the market economy. There was a common awareness of exhaustion, to the point where politics and social thought themselves seemed ludicrously out of date and naively ineffectual except as subjects of black comedy. Power everywhere seemed to have transformed itself from a forbidding line of troops into an ectoplasmic lump that simply swallowed up the righteous sword as it struck. Power was also doing its own, often surprising thing.

At least as an atmosphere, there was a not dissimilar disillusion in Eastern Europe and, for different reasons, in France too. As president of International PEN. I had the opportunity to move about in Eastern Europe, as well as in the Soviet Union, and I felt that local differences aside, intellectual life in the whole developed world had been stunned by a common failure to penetrate Power with a more humane and rational point of view. It may have been that the immense sense of relief and the high expectations that rushed in with the defeat of Hitler and Mussolini's fascism had to end in a letdown, but whatever the causes, by the seventies the rational seemed bankrupt as an ultimate sanction, a bar to which to appeal. And with it went a sense of history, even of the evolution of ideas and attitudes.

The ups and downs of disillusionment varied with time and place, however. It was possible to sit with Hungarian writers, for example, while they talked of a new liberalizing trend in their country, at the very moment that in Prague the depths of a merciless repression were being plumbed. There, with the Soviet ousting of Dubček and the crushing of all hope for an egalitarian socialist economy wedded to liberal freedoms of speech and artistic expression, the crash of expectations was especially terrible, for it was in Prague that this novel fusion seemed actually to have begun to function.

The seventies was also the era of the listening device, government's hidden bugs set in place to police the private conversations of its citizens—and not in Soviet areas alone. The White House was bugged, businesses were bugging competitors to defeat their strategies, and Watergate and the publication of the Pentagon Papers (which polls showed a majority of Americans disapproved) demonstrated that the Soviets had little to teach American presidents about domestic espionage. The burgling of psychiatrists' offices to spy out a government official's private life, the widespread bugging by political parties of each other's offices, all testified to the fact that the visible motions of political life were too often merely distractions, while the reality was what was happening in the dark.

Thus, when I found myself in Eastern European living rooms where it was all but absolutely certain that the walls or ceilings were bugged by the regime, it was not, disturbingly enough, an absolutely unfamiliar sensation for me. Of course there were very important differences—basically that an Eastern writer accused of seditious thoughts would have no appeal from his government's decision to hound him into silence, or worse. But the more I reflected on my experiences under bugged ceilings, the more the real issue changed from a purely political one to the question of what effect this surveillance was having on the minds of people who had to live under such ceilings, on whichever side of the Cold War line they happened to be.

Václav Havel, the Czech playwright who was later to serve a long term in prison, one day discovered a bug in his chandelier when house painters lowered it to paint the ceiling; deciding to deliver it to the local police, he said that it was government property that he did not think rightfully belonged to a private person. But the joke was as unappreciated as the eavesdropping itself was undenied. Very recently, in the home of a star Soviet writer, I began to convey the best wishes of a mutual friend, an émigré Russian novelist living in Europe, and the star motioned to me not to continue. Once outside, I asked if he wasn't depressed by having to live in a tapped house. He thought a moment, then shrugged—"I really don't know how I feel. I guess we figure the thing doesn't work!"—and burst out laughing at this jibe at Soviet inefficiency. Was he really all that unaffected by the presence of the unbidden guest? Perhaps so, but even if he had come to accept or at least abide it fatalistically, the bug's presence had changed him nonetheless. In my view it had perhaps dulled some resistance in him to Power's fingers ransacking his pockets every now and then. One learns to *include the bug* in the baggage of one's mind, in the calculus of one's plans and expectations, and this is not without effect.

The occasion, then, of *The Archbishop's Ceiling* is the bug and how people live with it, but the theme is something different. There are a number of adaptations to such a life: one man rails furiously at the ceiling, another questions that a bug is even up there, a third has changes of opinion from day to day; but man is so adaptable—and anyway the bug doesn't seem to be reacting much of the time and may simply be one more nuisance—that resistance to its presence is finally worn down to nothing. And that is when things become interesting, for something like the naked soul begins to loom, some essence in man that is simply unadaptable, ultimate, immutable as the horizon.

What, for instance, becomes of the idea of sincerity, the unmitigated expression of one's feelings and views, when one knows that Power's ear is most probably overhead? Is sincerity shaken by the sheer fact that one has so much as *taken the bug into consideration*? Under such pressure who can resist trying to some degree, however discreet and slight, to characterize himself for the benefit of the ceiling, whether as obedient conformist or even as resistant? And what, in that case, has been done to one's very identity? Does this process not overturn the very notion of an "I" in this kind of world? It would seem that "I" must be singular, not plural, but the art of bureaucracy is to change the "I" of its subjects to "we" at every moment of conscious life. What happens, in short, when people know that they are—at least most probably, if not certainly—at all times talking to Power, whether through a bug or a friend who is really an informer? Is it not something akin to accounting for oneself to a god? After all, most ideas of God see him as omnipresent, invisible, and condign in his judgments; the bug lacks only mercy and love to qualify, it is conscience shorn of moral distinctions.

In this play the most unreconcilable of the writers is clearly the most talented. Sigmund really has no permanent allegiance except to the love of creating art. Sigmund is also the most difficult to get along with, and has perhaps more than his share of cynicism and bitterness, narcissism and contempt for others. He is also choking with rage and love. In short, he is most alive, something that by itself would fuel his refusal—or constitutional incapacity—to accept the state's arrogant treatment. But with all his vitality, even he in the end must desperately call up a sanction, a sublime force beyond his ego, to sustain him in his opposition to that arrogance; for him it is the sublimity of art, in whose life-giving, creative essence he partakes and shares with other artists whose works he bows to, and in the act transcends the tyranny.

In a sense *Archbishop* begs the question of the existence of the sacred in the political life of man. But it begins to seem now that some kind of charmed circle has to be drawn around each person, across which the state may intrude only at its very real economic and political peril.

Glasnost, which did not exist in the seventies, is to the point here, for it is at bottom a Soviet attempt, born of economic crisis, to break up the perfection of its own social controls in order to open the channels of expression through which the creativity, the initiatives, and the improvisations of individual people may begin to flow and enrich the country. The problem, of course, is how to make this happen in a one-party state that in principle illegalizes opposition. But the wish is as plain as the desperate need of the economy itself, indeed of the regime, for the wisdom of the many and the release of their energies. Finally, the question arises whether, after so many generations of training in submission, the habits of open-minded inquiry and independence can be evoked in a sufficient number of people to make such a policy work.

Late in 1986, when glasnost was a brand-new idea scarcely taken seriously as the main thrust of the new administration, a Russian writer expressing the pre-glasnost view said to me, "What you people in the West don't understand is that we are not a competitive society and we don't wish to be. We want the government to protect us, that is what the government is for. When two Western writers meet, one of them most likely asks the other what he is writing now. Our writers never ask such a question. They are not competing. You have been in our Writers Union and seen those hundreds of writers going in and out, having their lunches, reading newspapers, writing letters, and so on. A big number of those people haven't written anything in years! Some perhaps wrote a few short stories or a novel some years ago—and that was it! They were made members of the Union, got the apartment and the vacation in the south, and it is not so different in any other field. But this is not such a terrible thing to us!"

But, I countered, there were surely some highly talented people who produced a good deal of work.

"Of course! But most are not so talented, so it's just as well they don't write too much anyway. But is it right that they should be thrown out in the streets to starve because they are not talented? We don't think so!"

What he had chosen to omit, of course, was that the mediocrities, of which he was all but admittedly one, usually run things in the Writers Union, something the gifted writers are usually too prickly and independent to be trusted to do. And so the system practically polices itself, stifling creativity and unpalatable truth-telling, and extolling the mediocre. But its main object, to contain any real attempts at change, is effectively secured. The only problem is that unless the system moves faster it may be permanently consigned to an inferior rank among the competing societies.

And so it may well have come to pass that the sanctity of the individual, his right to express his unique sense of reality freely and in public, has become an economic necessity and not alone a political or aesthetic and moral question. If that turns out to be the case, we will have been saved by a kind of economic morality based on necessity, the safest morality of all.

II

The American Clock was begun in the early seventies and did not reach final form until its production at the Mark Taper Forum in Los Angeles in 1984, a version that in turn was movingly and sometimes hilariously interpreted in the Peter Wood production two years later at the British National Theatre. The seemingly endless changes it went through reflected my own search for something like a dramatic resolution to what, after all, was one of the vaster social calamities in history—the Great Depression of the thirties. I have no hesitation in saying that as it now stands, the work is simply as close to such a resolution as I am able to bring it, just as the experience itself remains only partially resolved in the hands of historians. For the humiliating truth about any "period" is its essential chaos, about which any generalization can be no more than just that, a statement to which many exceptions may be taken.

With all its variety, however, there were certain features of the Depression era that set it apart, for they had not existed before in such force and over such a long time. One of the most important of these to me, both as a person living through those years and as a writer contemplating them three decades afterwards, was the introduction into the American psyche of a certain unprecedented *suspense*. Through the twenties the country, for me—and I believe I was typical—floated in a reassuring state of nature that merged boundlessly with the sea and the sky; I had never thought of it as even having a system. But the Crash forced us all to enter history willy-nilly, and everyone soon understood that there were other ways of conducting the nation's business—there simply had to be, because the one we had was so persistently not working. It was not only the radicals who were looking at the historical clock and asking how long our system could last, but people of every view-point. After all, they were hardly radicals who went to Washington to ask the newly inaugurated President Roosevelt to nationalize the banks, but bankers themselves who had finally confessed their inability to control their own system. The objective situation, in a word, had surfaced; people had taken on a new consciousness that had been rare in more prosperous times, and the alternatives of fascism or socialism were suddenly in the air.

Looking back at it all from the vantage of the early seventies, we seemed to have reinserted the old tabula rasa, the empty slate, into our heads again. Once more we were in a state of nature where no alternatives existed and nothing had grown out of anything else. Conservatism was still damning the liberal New Deal, yearning to dismantle its remaining prestige, but at the same time the Social Security system, unemployment and bank insurance, the regula-tory agencies in the stock market—the whole web of rational protections that the nation relied on—were products of the New Deal. We seemed to have lost awareness of community, of what we rightfully owe each other and what we owe ourselves. There seemed a want of any historical sense. America seems constantly in flight to the future; and it is a future made much like the past, a primeval paradise with really no government at all, in which the pioneer heads alone into the unknown forest to carve out his career. The suddenness of the '29 Crash and the chaos that followed offered a pure instance of the impotence of individualist solutions to so vast a crisis. As a society we learned all over again that we are in fact dependent and vulnerable, and that mass social organization does not necessarily weaken moral fiber but may set the stage for great displays of heroism and self-sacrifice and endurance. It may also unleash, as it did in the thirties, a flood of humor and optimism that was far less apparent in seemingly happier years.

When Studs Terkel's *Hard Times* appeared in 1970, the American economy was booming, and it would be another seventeen years before the stock market collapsed to anything like the degree it had in 1929. In any case, in considering his collection of interviews with survivors of the Depression as a partial basis for a play (I would mix my own memories into it as well), I had no prophecy of doom in mind, although in sheer principle it seemed impossible that the market could keep on rising indefinitely. At bottom, quite simply, I wanted to try to show how it was and where we had come from. I wanted to give some sense of life as we lived it when the clock was ticking every day.

The idea was not, strictly speaking, my invention but a common notion of the thirties. And it was a concept that also extended outward to Europe and the Far East; Hitler was clearly preparing to destroy parliamentary governments as soon he organized his armies, just as Franco had destroyed the Spanish Republic, and Japan was manifestly creating a new empire that must one day collide with the interests of Britain and the United States. The clock was ticking everywhere.

Difficulties with the play had to do almost totally with finding a balance between the epic elements and the intimate psychological lives of individuals and families like the Baums. My impulse is usually toward integration of meaning through significant individual action, but the striking new fact of life in the Depression era—unlike the self-sufficient, prosperous seventies—was the swift rise in the common consciousness of the social system. Uncharacteristically, Americans were looking for answers far beyond the bedroom and purely personal relationships, and so the very form of the play should ideally reflect this wider awareness. But how to unify the two elements, objective and subjective, epic and psychological? The sudden and novel impact of the Depression made people in the cities, for example, painfully conscious that thousands of farm families were being forced off their lands in the West by a combination of a collapsed market for farm goods and the unprecedented drought and dust storms. The farmers who remained operating were aware—and openly resentful—that in the cities people could not afford to buy the milk for which they could not get commercially viable prices. The social paradoxes of the collapse were so glaring that it would be false to the era to try to convey its spirit through the life of any one family. Nevertheless the feeling of a unified theatrical event evaded me until the revision for the 1984 Mark Taper production, which I believe came close to striking the balance. But it was in the British National Theatre production two years later that the play's theatrical life was finally achieved. The secret was vaudeville.

Of course the period had much tragedy and was fundamentally a trial and a frustration for those who lived through it, but no time ever created so many comedians and upbeat songs. Jack Benny, Fred Allen, W. C. Fields, Jimmy Durante, Eddie Cantor, Burns and Allen, and Ed Wynn were some of the headliners who came up in that time, and the song lyrics were most often exhilaratingly optimistic: "Love Is Sweeping the Country," "Life Is Just a Bowl of Cherries," "April in Paris," "I'm Getting Sentimental over You," "Who's Afraid of the Big Bad Wolf?" It was, in the pop culture, a romantic time and not at all realistically harsh. The serious writers were putting out books like Nathanael West's *Miss Lonelyhearts*, Erskine Caldwell's *God's Little Acre*, Jack Conroy's

The Disinherited, André Malraux's *Man's Fate*, Hemingway's *Winner Take Nothing*, and Steinbeck's *In Dubious Battle*, and Edward Hopper was brooding over his stark street scenes, and Reginald Marsh was painting vagrants asleep in the subways, but Broadway had O'Neill's first comedy, *Ah, Wilderness!*, and another comical version of the hard life, *Tobacco Road*, Noel Coward's *Design for Living*, the Gershwins' *Let 'Em Eat Cake*, and some of the best American farces ever written—*Room Service, Three Men on a Horse*, and *Brother Rat* among them.

In the Mark Taper production I found myself allowing the material to move through me as it wished—I had dozens of scenes by this time and was shifting them about in search of their hidden emotional as well as ideational linkages. At one point the experience brought to mind a sort of vaudeville where the contiguity of sublime and ridiculous is perfectly acceptable; in vaudeville an imitation of Lincoln doing the Gettysburg Address could easily be followed by Chinese acrobats. So when subsequently Peter Wood asked for my feeling about the style, I could call the play a vaudeville with an assurance born of over a decade of experimentation. He took the hint and ran with it, tossing up the last shreds of a realistic approach, announcing from the opening image that the performance was to be epic and declarative.

Out of darkness, in a brash music hall spotlight, a baseball pitcher appears and tosses a ball from hand to glove as he gets ready on the mound. The other characters saunter on singing snatches of songs of the thirties, and from somewhere in the balcony a man in a boater and striped shirt, bow tie and gartered sleeves—Ted Quinn—whistles "I Found a Million-Dollar Baby in a Five-and-Ten-Cent Store." At one side of the open stage, a five-piece jazz band plays in full view of the audience (impossible in the penurious New York theatre), and the sheer festivity of the occasion is already established.

The most startling, and I think wonderful, invention of all was the treatment of the character of Theodore K. Quinn. This was the actual name of a neighbor of mine, son of a Chicago railroad labor organizer, who had worked himself up from a poor Chicago law student to the vice-presidency of General Electric. The president of GE, Quinn's boss through most of the twenties, was Gerard Swope, a world-famous capitalist and much quoted social thinker, who decided as the thirties dawned that Quinn was to succeed him on his retirement. Quinn, in charge of the consumer products division of the company, had frequently bought up promising smaller manufacturers for Swope, incorporating their plants into the GE giant, but had developed a great fear that this process of cartelization must end in the destruction of democracy itself. Over the years his rationalization had been that he was only taking orders—although in fact it was on his judgment that Swope depended as to which companies to pick up. Then the excuses were threatened by his elevation to the presidency, an office with dictatorial powers at the time. As he would tell me, "Above the president of General Electric stood only God."

The real Ted Quinn had actually been president of GE for a single day, at the end of which he put in his resignation. "I just couldn't stand being the Lord High Executioner himself," he once said to me. He went on to open an advisory service for small businesses and made a good fortune at it. During World War II he was a dollar-a-year head of the Small Business Administration in Washington, seeing to it that the giant concerns did not gobble up all the available steel. Particularly close to his heart was the Amana company, a cooperative.

Quinn also published several books, including *Giant Business, Threat to Democracy* and *Unconscious Public Enemies,* his case against GE-type monopolies. These, along with his anti-monopoly testimony before congressional committees, got him obliterated from the roster of former GE executives, and the company actually denied—to journalist Matthew Josephson, who at my behest made an inquiry in 1972—that he had ever so much as worked for GE. However, in the course of time a film director friend of mine who loved to browse in flea markets and old bookstores came on a leather-covered daily diary put out by GE as a gift for its distributors, circa 1930, in which the company directors are listed, and Theodore K. Quinn is right there as vice-president for consumer sales. The fact is that it was he who, among a number of other innovations, conceived of the compact electric refrigerator as a common consumer product, at a time when electric refrigeration was regarded as a purely commercial item, the behemoth used in restaurants, hotels, and the kitchens of wealthy estates.

From the big business viewpoint Quinn's central heresy was that democracy basically depended on a large class of independent entrepreneurs who would keep the market competitive. His fear was that monopoly, which he saw spreading in the American economy despite superficial appearances of competition, would end by crippling the system's former ingenuity and its capacity to produce high-quality goods at reasonable prices. A monopoly has little need to improve its product when it has little need to compete. (First Communist China and then Gorbachev's Russia would be grappling with a very similar dilemma in the years to come.) He loved to reel off a long list of inventions, from the jet engine to the zipper, that were devised by independent inventors rather than corporations and their much advertised laboratories: "The basic things we use and are famous for were conceived in the back of a garage." I knew him in the fifties, when his populist vision was totally out of fashion, and maybe, I feared, an out-of-date relic of a bygone America. But I would hear it again in the seventies and even more loudly in the eighties as a muscle-bound American industrial machine, wallowing for generations in a continental market beyond the reach of foreign competition, was caught flat-footed by German and Japanese competitors. Quinn was a successful businessman interested in money and production, but his vision transcended the market to embrace the nature of the democratic system for which he had a passion, and which he thought doomed if Americans did not understand the real threats to it. He put it starkly once: "It may be all over, I don't know—but I don't want to have to choose between fascism and socialism, because neither one can match a really free, competitive economy and the political liberties it makes possible. If I do have to choose, it'll be socialism, because it harms the people less. But neither one is the way I'd want to go."

Perhaps it was because the style of the National Theatre production was so unashamed in its presentational declarativeness that the Ted Quinn role was given to David Schofield, a tap dancer with a brash Irish mug, for Quinn was forever bragging about—and mocking—his mad love of soft-shoe dancing. And so we had long speeches about the dire consequences of business monopoly delivered by a dancer uncorking a most ebullient soft-shoe all over the stage, supported by some witty jazz played openly before our eyes by a deft band. As Quinn agonizes over whether to accept the presidency of GE, a phone rings at the edge of the stage; plainly, it is as the new president that he must answer it. He taps his way over to it, lifts the receiver, and simply places it gently on the floor and dances joyously away.

It was in the National Theatre that I at last heard the right kind of straightforward epic expressiveness, joyful and celebratory rather than abashed and veiled, as economic and political—which is to say epic—subjects were in the mouths of the characters. In this antic yet thematically precise spirit, accompanied by some forty songs out of the period, the show managed to convey the *seriousness* of the disaster that the Great Depression was, and at the same time its human heart.

There was one more invention that I particularly prized. Alone in her Brooklyn house, Rose Baum sits at the piano, bewildered and discouraged by the endless Depression, and plays some of the popular ballads of the day, breaking off now and then to muse to herself about the neighborhood, the country, her family, her fading hopes. The actress sat at a piano whose keyboard faced the audience, and simply held her hands suspended over the keys while the band pianist a few yards away played the romantic thirties tunes. Gradually a triple reality formed such as I have rarely witnessed in the theatre: first, the objective stage reality of the band pianist playing, but somehow magically directed by Rose's motionless hands over her keyboard; and simultaneously, *the play's memory* of this lost past that we are now discovering again; and finally, the middle-aged actress herself seeming, by virtue of her motionless hands suspended over the keys, to be recalling this moment from her very own life. The style, in short, had fused emotion and conscious awareness, overt intention and subjective feeling—the aim in view from the beginning, more than a decade before.

The Archbishop's Ceiling

CHARACTERS

ADRIAN
MAYA
MARCUS
IRINA
SIGMUND

ACT ONE

Some time ago.

A capital in Europe; the sitting room in the former residence of the archbishop.

Judging by the depth of the casement around the window at right, the walls must be two feet thick. The room has weight and power, its contents chaotic and sensuous. Decoration is early baroque.

The ceiling is first seen: in high relief the Four Winds, cheeks swelling, and cherubim, darkened unevenly by soot and age.

Light is from a few lamps of every style, from a contemporary bridge lamp to something that looks like an electrified hookah, but the impression of a dark, overcrowded room remains; the walls absorb light.

A grand piano, scarved; a large blue vase on the floor under it.

Unhung paintings, immense and dark, leaning against a wall, in heavy gilt frames.

Objects of dull brass not recently polished.

Two or three long, dark carved chests topped with tasseled rose-colored cushions.

A long, desiccated brown leather couch with billowing cushions; a stately carved armchair, bolsters, Oriental camel bags.

A pink velour settee, old picture magazines piled on its foot and underneath—Life, Stern, Europeo . . .

A Bauhaus chair in chrome and black leather on one of the smallish Persian rugs.

3

A wide, ornate rolltop desk, probably out of the twenties, with a stuffed falcon or gamebird on its top.

Contemporary books on shelves, local classics in leather.

A sinuous chaise in faded pink.

Layers of chaos.

At up right a doorway to the living quarters.

At left a pair of heavy doors opening on a dimly lit corridor. More chests here, a few piled-up chairs. This corridor leads upstage into darkness (and the unseen stairway down to the front door). The corridor wall is of large unfaced stones.

ADRIAN is seated on a couch. He is relaxed, in an attitude of waiting, legs crossed, arms spread wide. Now he glances at the doorway to the living quarters, considers for a moment, then lifts up the couch cushions, looking underneath. He stands and goes to a table lamp, tilts it over to look under its base. He looks about again and peers into the open piano.

He glances up at the doorway again, then examines the ceiling, his head turned straight up. With another glance at the doorway he proceeds to the window at right and looks behind the drapes.

MAYA enters from the living quarters with a coffeepot and two cups on a tray.

ADRIAN: Tremendous view of the city from up here.

MAYA: Yes.

ADRIAN: Like seeing it from a plane. Or a dream. (*He turns and approaches the couch, blows on his hands.*)

MAYA: Would you like one of his sweaters? I'm sorry there's no firewood.

ADRIAN: It's warm enough. He doesn't heat this whole house, does he?

MAYA: It's impossible—only this and the bedroom. But the rest of it's never used.

ADRIAN: I forgot how gloomy it is in here.

MAYA: It's a hard room to light. Wherever you put a lamp it makes the rest seem darker. I think there are too many unrelated objects—the eye can't rest here. (*She laughs, offers a cup; he takes it.*)

ADRIAN: Thanks, Maya. (*He sits.*) Am I interrupting something?

MAYA: I never do anything. When did you arrive?

ADRIAN: Yesterday morning. I was in Paris.

MAYA: And how long do you stay?

ADRIAN: Maybe tomorrow night—I'll see.

MAYA: So short!

ADRIAN: I had a sudden yen to come look around again, see some of the fellows. And you.

MAYA: They gave a visa so quickly?

ADRIAN: Took two days.

MAYA: How wonderful to be famous.

ADRIAN: I was surprised I got one at all—I've attacked them, you know.

MAYA: In the *New York Times*.

ADRIAN: Oh, you read it.

MAYA: Last fall, I believe.

ADRIAN: What'd you think of it?

MAYA: It was interesting. I partly don't remember. I was surprised you did journalism. (*She sips. He waits; nothing more.*)

ADRIAN: I wonder if they care what anybody writes about them anymore.

MAYA: Yes, they do—very much, I think. But I really don't know. . . . How's your wife?

ADRIAN: Ruth? She's good.

MAYA: I liked her. She had a warm heart. I don't like many women.

ADRIAN: You look different.

MAYA: I'm two years older—and three kilos.

ADRIAN: It becomes you.

MAYA: Too fat.

ADRIAN: No . . . *zaftig*. You look creamy. You changed your hairdo.

MAYA: From *Vogue* magazine.

ADRIAN (*laughs*): That so! It's sporty.

MAYA: What brings you back?

ADRIAN: . . . Your English is a thousand percent better. More colloquial.

MAYA: I recite aloud from *Vogue* magazine.

ADRIAN: You're kidding.

MAYA: Seriously. Is all I read anymore.

ADRIAN: Oh, go on with you.

MAYA: Everything in *Vogue* magazine is true.

ADRIAN: Like the girl in pantyhose leaning on her pink Rolls-Royce.

MAYA: Oh, yes, is marvelous. One time there was a completely naked girl in a mink coat (*she extends her foot*) and one foot touching the bubble bath. Fantastic imagination. It is the only modern art that really excites me.

ADRIAN *laughs.*

And their expressions, these girls. Absolutely nothing. Like the goddesses of the Greeks—beautiful, stupid, everlasting. This magazine is classical.

ADRIAN: You're not drinking anymore?

MAYA: Only after nine o'clock.

ADRIAN: Good. You seem more organized.

MAYA: Until nine o'clock.

They laugh. MAYA *sips. Slight pause.* ADRIAN *sips.*

ADRIAN: What's Marcus doing in London?

MAYA: His last novel is coming out there just now.

ADRIAN: That's nice. I hear it was a success here.

MAYA: Very much—you say very much or . . . ?

ADRIAN: Very much so.

MAYA: Very much so—what a language!

ADRIAN: You're doing great. You must practice a lot.

MAYA: Only when the English come to visit Marcus, or the Americans. . . . I have his number in London if you . . .

ADRIAN: I have nothing special to say to him.

Pause.

MAYA: You came back for one day?

ADRIAN: Well, three, really. I was in a symposium at the Sorbonne—about the contemporary novel—and it got so pompous I got an urge to sit down again with writers who had actual troubles. So I thought I'd stop by before I went home.

MAYA: You've seen anyone?

ADRIAN: Yes. (*Slight pause. He reaches for a pack of cigarettes.*)

MAYA (*turning to him quickly, to forgive his not elaborating*): It's all right . . .

ADRIAN: I had dinner with Otto and Sigmund and their wives.

MAYA (*surprised*): Oh! You should have called me.

ADRIAN: I tried three times.

MAYA: But Sigmund knows my number.

ADRIAN: You don't live here anymore?

MAYA: Only when Marcus is away. (*She indicates the bedroom doorway.*) He has that tremendous bathtub . . .

ADRIAN: I remember, yes. When'd you break up?

MAYA: I don't remember—eight or nine months, I think. We are friends. Sigmund didn't tell you?

ADRIAN: Nothing. Maybe 'cause his wife was there.

MAYA: Why? I am friends with Elizabeth. . . . So you have a new novel, I suppose.

ADRIAN (*laughs*): You make it sound like I have one every week.

MAYA: I always think you write so easily.

ADRIAN: I always have. But I just abandoned one that I worked on for two years. I'm still trying to get up off the floor. I forgot how easy you are to talk to.

MAYA: But you seem nervous.

ADRIAN: Just sexual tension.

MAYA: You wanted to make love tonight?

ADRIAN: If it came to it, sure. (*He takes her hand.*) In Paris we were in the middle of a discussion of Marxism and surrealism, and I suddenly got this blinding vision of the inside of your thigh . . .

She laughs, immensely pleased.

. . . so I'm here. (*He leans over and kisses her on the lips. Then he stands.*) Incidentally . . . Ruth and I never married, you know.

MAYA (*surprised*): But didn't you call each other . . .

ADRIAN: We never did, really, but we never bothered to correct people. It just made it easier to travel and live together.

MAYA: And now?

ADRIAN: We're apart together. I want my own fireplace, but with a valid plane ticket on the mantel.

MAYA: Well, that's natural, you're a man.

ADRIAN: In my country I'm a child and a son of a bitch. But I'm toying with the idea of growing up—I may ask her to marry me.

MAYA: Is that necessary?

ADRIAN: You're a smart girl—that's exactly the question.

MAYA: Whether it is necessary.

ADRIAN: Not exactly that—few books are necessary; a writer has to write. It's that it became absurd, suddenly. Here I'm laying out motives, characterizations, secret impulses—the whole psychological chess game—when the truth is I'm not sure anymore that I believe in psychology. That anything we think really determines what we're going to do. Or even what we feel. This interest you?

MAYA: You mean anyone can do anything.

ADRIAN: Almost. Damn near. But the point is a little different. Ruth—when we came back from here two years ago—she went into a terrible depression. She'd had them before, but this time she seemed suicidal.

MAYA: Oh, my God. Why?

ADRIAN: Who knows? There were so many reasons there was no reason. She went back to psychiatry. Other therapies . . . nothing worked. Finally, they gave her a pill. (*Slight pause.*) It was miraculous. Turned her completely around. She's full of energy, purpose, optimism. Looks five years younger.

MAYA: A chemical.

ADRIAN: Yes. She didn't have the psychic energy to pull her stockings up. Now they've just made her assistant to the managing editor of her magazine. Does fifty laps a day in the swimming pool— It plugged her in to some . . . some power. And she lit up.

MAYA: She is happy?

ADRIAN: I don't really know—she doesn't talk about her mind anymore, her soul; she talks about what she does. Which is terrific . . .

MAYA: But boring.

ADRIAN: In a way, maybe—but you can't knock it; I really think it saved her life. But what bothers me is something else. (*Slight pause.*) She knows neither more nor less about herself now than when she was trying to die. The interior landscape has not lit up. What has changed is her reaction to power. Before she feared it, now she enjoys it. Before she fled from it, now she seeks it. She got plugged in, and she's come alive.

MAYA: So you have a problem.

ADRIAN: What problem do you think I have?

MAYA: It is unnecessary to write novels anymore.

ADRIAN: God, you're smart—yes. It made me think of Hamlet. Here we are tracking that marvelous maze of his mind, but isn't that slightly ludicrous when one knows that with the right pill his anxiety would dissolve? Christ, he's got everything to live for, heir to the throne, servants, horses—correctly medicated, he could have made a deal with the king and married Ophelia. Or Socrates—instead of hemlock, a swig of lithium and he'd end up the mayor of Athens and live to a hundred. What is lost? Some wisdom, some knowledge found in suffering. But knowledge is power, that's why it's good—so what is wrong with gaining power without having to suffer at all?

MAYA (*with the faintest color of embarrassment, it seems*): You have some reason to ask me this question?

ADRIAN: Yes.

MAYA: Why?

ADRIAN: You have no pills in this country, but power is very sharply defined here. The government makes it very clear that you must snuggle up to power or you will never be happy. (*Slight pause.*) I'm wondering what that does to people, Maya. Does it smooth them all out when they know they must all plug in or their lights go out, regardless of what they think or their personalities?

MAYA: I have never thought of this question. (*She glances at her watch.*) I am having a brandy, will you? (*She stands.*)

ADRIAN (*laughs*): It's nine o'clock?

MAYA: In one minute. (*She goes upstage, pours.*)

ADRIAN: I'd love one; thanks.

MAYA: But I have another mystery. (*She carefully pours two*

glasses. He waits. She brings him one, remains standing.)
Cheers.

ADRIAN: Cheers. (*They drink.*) Wow—that's good.

MAYA: I prefer whisky, but he locks it up when he is away. (*She sits apart from him.*) I have known intimately so many writers; they all write books condemning people who wish to be successful and praised, who desire some power in life. But I have never met one writer who did not wish to be praised and successful . . . (*she is smiling*) . . . and even powerful. Why do they condemn others who wish the same for themselves?

ADRIAN: Because they understand them so well.

MAYA: For this reason I love *Vogue* magazine.

    He laughs.

I am serious. In this magazine everyone is successful. No one has ever apologized because she was beautiful and happy. I believe this magazine. (*She knocks back the remains of her drink, stands, goes toward the liquor upstage.*) Tell me the truth—why have you come back?

ADRIAN (*slight pause*): You think I could write a book about this country?

MAYA (*brings down the bottle, fills his glass*): No, Adrian.

ADRIAN: I'm too American.

MAYA: No, the Russians cannot either. (*She refills her own glass.*) A big country cannot understand small possibilities. When it is raining in Moscow, the sun is shining in Tashkent. Terrible snow in New York, but it is a beautiful day in Arizona. In a small country, when it rains it rains everywhere. (*She sits beside him.*) Why have you come back?

ADRIAN: I've told you.

MAYA: Such a trip—for three days?

ADRIAN: Why not? I'm rich.

MAYA (*examines his face*): You are writing a book about us.

ADRIAN: I've written it, and abandoned it. I want to write it again.

MAYA: About this country.

ADRIAN: About you.

MAYA: But what do you know about me?

ADRIAN: Practically nothing. But something in me knows everything.

MAYA: I am astonished.

ADRIAN: My visa's good through the week—I'll stay if we could spend a lot of time together. Could we? It'd mean a lot to me.

An instant. She gets up, goes to a drawer, and takes out a new pack of cigarettes.

I promise nobody'll recognize you—the character is blonde and very tall and has a flat chest. What do you say?

MAYA: But why?

ADRIAN: I've become obsessed with this place, it's like some Jerusalem for me.

MAYA: But we are of no consequence . . .

ADRIAN: Neither is Jerusalem, but it always has to be saved. Let me stay here with you till Friday. When is Marcus coming back?

MAYA: I never know—not till spring, probably. Is he also in your book?

ADRIAN: In a way. Don't be mad, I swear you won't be recognized.

MAYA: You want me to talk about him?

ADRIAN: I'd like to understand him, that's all.

MAYA: For example?

ADRIAN: Well . . . let's see. You know, I've run into Marcus in three or four countries the past five years; had long talks together, but when I go over them in my mind I realize he's never said anything at all about himself. I like him, always glad to see him, but he's a total blank. For instance, how does he manage to get a house like this?

MAYA: But why not?

ADRIAN: It belongs to the government, doesn't it?

MAYA: It is the same way he gets everything—his trips abroad, his English suits, his girls . . .

ADRIAN: How?

MAYA: He assumes he deserves them.

ADRIAN: But his money—he seems to have quite a lot.

MAYA (*shrugs, underplaying the fact*): He sells his father's books from time to time. He had a medieval collection . . .

ADRIAN: They don't confiscate such things?

MAYA: Perhaps they haven't thought of it. You are the only person I know who thinks everything in a Socialist country is rational.

ADRIAN: In other words, Marcus is a bit of an operator.

MAYA: Marcus? Marcus is above all naive.

ADRIAN: Naive! You don't mean that.

MAYA: No one but a naive man spends six years in prison, Adrian.

ADRIAN: But in that period they were arresting everybody, weren't they?

MAYA: By no means everybody. Marcus is rather a brave man.

ADRIAN: Huh! I had him all wrong. What do you say, let me bring my bag over.

MAYA: You have your book with you?

ADRIAN: No, it's home.

She seems skeptical.

. . . Why would I carry it with me?

She stares at him with the faintest smile.

What's happening?

MAYA: I don't know—what do you think?

She gets up, cradling her glass, walks thoughtfully to another seat, and sits. He gets up and comes to her.

ADRIAN: What is it?

She shakes her head. She seems overwhelmed by some wider sadness. His tone now is uncertain.

Maya?

MAYA: You've been talking to Allison Wolfe?

ADRIAN: I've talked to him, yes.

She stands, moves, comes to a halt.

MAYA: He is still telling that story?

ADRIAN (*slight pause*): I didn't believe him, Maya.

MAYA: He's a vile gossip.

ADRIAN: He's a writer. All writers are gossips.

MAYA: He is a vile man.

ADRIAN: I didn't believe him.

MAYA: What did he say to you?

ADRIAN: Why go into it?

MAYA: I want to know. Please.

ADRIAN: It was ridiculous, I know that. Allison has a puritan imagination.

MAYA: Tell me what he said.

ADRIAN (*slight pause*): Well . . . that you and Marcus . . . look, it's so stupid . . .

MAYA: That we have orgies here?

ADRIAN: . . . Yes.

MAYA: And we bring in young girls?

He is silent.

Adrian?

ADRIAN: That this house is bugged. And you bring in girls to compromise writers with the government.

Pause.

MAYA: You'd better go, I believe.

He is silent for a moment, observing her. She is full.

I'm tired anyway . . . I was just going to bed when you called.

ADRIAN: Maya, if I believed it, would I have talked as I have in here?

MAYA (*smiling*): I don't know, Adrian—would you? Anyway, you have your passport. Why not?

ADRIAN: You know I understand the situation too well to believe Allison. Resistance is impossible anymore. I know the government's got the intellectuals in its pocket, and the few who aren't have stomach ulcers. (*He comes to her, takes her hand.*) I *was* nervous when I came in, but it was sexual tension—I knew we'd be alone.

Her suspicion remains; she slips her hand out of his.

. . . All right, I did think of it. But that's inevitable, isn't it?

MAYA: Yes, of course. (*She moves away again.*)

ADRIAN: It's hard for anyone to know what to believe in this country, you can understand that.

MAYA: Yes. (*She sits, lonely.*)

ADRIAN (*sits beside her*): Forgive me, will you?

MAYA: It is terrible.

ADRIAN: What do you say we forget it?

She looks at him with uncertainty.

What are you doing now?

Slight pause. She stares front for a moment, then takes a breath as though resolving to carry on. Her tone brightens.

MAYA: I write for the radio.

ADRIAN: No plays anymore?

MAYA: I can't work that hard anymore.

ADRIAN: They wouldn't put them on?

MAYA: Oh, they would—I was never political, Adrian.

ADRIAN: You were, my first time . . .

MAYA: Well, everybody was in those days. But it wasn't really politics.

ADRIAN: What, then?

MAYA: I don't know—some sort of illusion that we could be Communists without having enemies. It was a childishness, dancing around the Maypole. It could never last, life is not like that.

ADRIAN: What do you write?

MAYA: I broadcast little anecdotes, amusing things I notice on the streets, the trams. I am on once a week; they have me on Saturday mornings for breakfast. What is it you want to know?

ADRIAN: I'm not interviewing you, Maya.

MAYA (*stands suddenly, between anger and fear*): Why have you come?

ADRIAN (*stands*): I've told you, Maya—I thought maybe I could grab hold of the feeling again.

MAYA: Of what?

ADRIAN: This country, this situation. It escapes me the minute I cross the border. It's like some goddamned demon that only lives here.

MAYA: But we are only people, what is so strange?

ADRIAN: I'll give you an example. It's an hour from Paris here; we sit down to dinner last night in a restaurant, and two plain-clothesmen take the next table. It was blatant. Not the slightest attempt to disguise that they were there to intimidate Sigmund and Otto. They kept staring straight at them.

MAYA: But why did he take you to a restaurant? Elizabeth could have given you dinner.

ADRIAN: . . . I don't understand.

MAYA: But Sigmund knows that will happen if he walks about with a famous American writer.

ADRIAN: You're not justifying it? . . .

MAYA: I have not been appointed to justify or condemn anything. (*She laughs.*) And neither has Sigmund. He is an artist, a very great writer, and that is what he should be doing.

ADRIAN: I can't believe what I'm hearing, Maya.

MAYA (*laughs*): But you must, Adrian. You really must believe it.

ADRIAN: You mean it's perfectly all right for two cops to be . . .

MAYA: But that is their *business*. But it is not Sigmund's business to be taunting the government. Do you go about trying to infuriate your CIA, your FBI?

   He is silent.

Of course not. You stay home and write your books. Just as the Russian writers stay home and write theirs . . .

ADRIAN: But Sigmund isn't permitted to write his books . . .

MAYA: My God—don't you understand *anything*?

   The sudden force of her outburst is mystifying to him. He looks at her, perplexed. She gathers herself.

I'm very tired, Adrian. Perhaps we can meet again before you leave.

ADRIAN: Okay. (*He looks about.*) I forgot where I put my coat . . .

MAYA: I hung it inside.

   She goes upstage and out through the doorway. ADRIAN, *his face taut, looks around at the room, up at the ceiling. She returns, hands him the coat.*

You know your way back to the hotel?

ADRIAN: I'll find it. (*He extends his hand, she takes it.*) I'm not as simple as I seem, Maya.

MAYA: I'm sorry I got excited.

ADRIAN: I understand—you don't want him taking risks.

MAYA: Why should he? Especially when things are improving all the time anyway.

ADRIAN: They aren't arresting anybody? . . .

MAYA: Of course not. Sigmund just can't get himself to admit it, so he does these stupid things. One can live as peacefully as anywhere.

ADRIAN (*putting on his coat*): Still, it's not every country where writers keep a novel manuscript behind their fireplace.

MAYA (*stiffening*): Good night.

ADRIAN (*sees her cooled look; slight pause*): Good night, Maya. (*He crosses the room to the double doors at left, and as he opens one . . .*)

MAYA: Adrian?

He turns in the doorway.

You didn't really mean that, I hope.

He is silent. She turns to him.

No one keeps manuscripts behind a fireplace anymore. You know that.

ADRIAN (*looks at her for a moment, with irony*): . . . Right. (*He stands there, hand on the door handle, looking down at the floor, considering. He smiles, turning back to her.*) Funny how life imitates art; the melodrama kept flattening out my characterizations. It's an interesting problem—whether it matters who anyone is or what anyone thinks, when all that counts anymore—is power.

He goes brusquely into the corridor, walks upstage into dark-

ness. She hesitates, then rushes out, closing the door behind her, and calls up the corridor.

MAYA (*a suppressed call*): Adrian? (*She waits.*) Adrian!

He reappears from the darkness and stands shaking his head, angry and appalled. She has stiffened herself against her confession.

We can talk out here, it is only in the apartment.

ADRIAN: Jesus Christ, Maya.

MAYA: I want you to come inside for a moment—you should not have mentioned Sigmund's manuscript . . .

ADRIAN (*stunned, a look of disgust—adopting her muffled tone*): Maya . . . how can you do this?

MAYA (*with an indignant note*): They never knew he has written a novel, how dare you mention it! Did he give it to you?

ADRIAN: My head is spinning, what the hell is this? . . .

MAYA: Did he give it to you?

ADRIAN (*a flare of open anger*): How can I tell you anything? . . .

MAYA: Come inside. Say that you have sent it to Paris. Come . . . (*She starts for the door.*)

ADRIAN: How the hell would I send it to Paris?

MAYA: They'll be searching his house now, they'll destroy it! You must say that you sent it today with some friend of yours. (*She pulls him by the sleeve.*)

ADRIAN (*freeing himself*): Wait a minute—you mean they were taping us in bed?

MAYA: I don't know. I don't know when it was installed. Please . . . simply say that you have sent the manuscript to Paris. Come. (*She grasps the door handle.*)

ADRIAN (*stepping back from the door*): That's a crime.

> *She turns to him with a contemptuous look.*

Well, it is, isn't it? Anyway, I didn't say it was his book.

MAYA: It was obviously him. Say you have sent it out! You must! (*She opens the door instantly and enters the room, speaking in a relaxed, normal tone.*) . . . Perhaps you'd better stay until the rain lets up. I might go to bed, but why don't you make yourself comfortable?

ADRIAN (*hesitates in the corridor, then enters the room and stands there in silence, glancing about*): . . . All right. Thanks. (*He stands there, silent, in his fear.*)

MAYA: Yes?

ADRIAN: Incidentally— (*He breaks off. A long hiatus. He is internally positioning himself to the situation.*) . . . that manuscript I mentioned.

MAYA: Yes?

ADRIAN: It's in Paris by now. I . . . gave it to a friend who was leaving this morning.

MAYA: Oh?

ADRIAN: Yes. (*Slight pause. It occurs to him suddenly:*) A girl.

MAYA (*as though amused*): You already have girls here?

ADRIAN (*starting to grin*): Well, not really—she's a cousin of mine. Actually, a second cousin. Just happened to meet her on the street. All right if I have another brandy?

MAYA: Of course.

ADRIAN (*pours*): I'll be going in a minute. (*He sits in his coat on the edge of a chair with his glass.*) Just let me digest this. This drink, I mean.

She sits on the edge of another chair a distance away.

Quite an atmosphere in this house. I never realized it before.

MAYA: It's so old. Sixteenth century, I think.

ADRIAN: It's so alive—once you're aware of it.

MAYA: They built very well in those days.

ADRIAN (*directly to her*): Incredible. I really didn't believe it.

MAYA: Please go.

ADRIAN: In one minute. Did I dream it, or did it belong to the archbishop?

MAYA: It was his residence.

ADRIAN (*looks up to the ceiling*): That explains the cherubims . . . (*looks at his drink*) . . . and the antonyms.

She stands.

I'm going. This is . . . (*looks around*) . . . this is what I never got into my book—this doubleness. This density with angels hovering overhead. Like power always with you in a room. Like God, in a way. Just tell me—do you ever get where you've forgotten it?

MAYA: I don't really live here anymore.

ADRIAN: Why? You found this style oppressive?

MAYA: I don't hear the rain. Please.

ADRIAN (*stands facing her*): I'm not sure I should, but I'm filling up with sympathy. I'm sorry as hell, Maya.

She is silent.

I could hire a car—let's meet for lunch and take a drive in the country.

MAYA: All right. I'll pick you up at the hotel. (*She starts past him toward the doors.*)

ADRIAN (*takes her hand as she passes*): Thirty seconds. Please. I want to chat. Just to hear myself. (*He moves her to a chair.*) Half a minute . . . just in case you don't show up.

MAYA (*sitting*): Of course I will.

ADRIAN (*clings to her hand, kneebends before her*): I've never asked you before—you ever been married?

   She laughs.

Come on, give me a chat. Were you?

MAYA: Never, no.

ADRIAN: And what were your people—middle class?

MAYA: Workers. They died of flu in the war.

ADRIAN: Who brought you up?

MAYA: The nuns.

ADRIAN (*stands; looks around*): . . . Is it always like a performance? Like we're quoting ourselves?

MAYA (*stands*): Goodnight. (*She goes and opens the door.*)

ADRIAN: My God—you poor girl. (*He takes her into his arms and kisses her.*) Maybe I should say—in all fairness—(*leaving her, he addresses the ceiling*) that the city looks much cleaner than my last time. And there's much more stuff in the shops. And the girls have shaved their legs. In fact—(*he turns to her—she is smiling*) this is the truth—I met my dentist in the hotel this morning. He's crazy about this country! (*With a wild underlay of laughter:*) Can't get over the way he can walk the streets any hour of the night, which is impossible in New York. Said he'd never felt so relaxed and free in his whole life! And at that very instant, Sigmund and Otto walked into the lobby, and he congratulated them on having such a fine up-and-coming little civilization! (*He suddenly yells at the top of his lungs.*) Forgive me, I scream in New York sometimes.

She is half smiling, alert to him; he comes to the open doorway and grasps her hands.

Goodnight. And if I never see you again . . .

MAYA: I'll be there, why not?

ADRIAN: How do I know? But just in case—I want you to know that I'll never forget you in that real short skirt you wore last time, and the moment when you slung one leg over the arm of the chair. You have a sublime sluttishness, Maya—don't be mad, it's a gift when it's sublime.

She laughs.

How marvelous to see you laugh—come, walk me downstairs. (*He pulls her through the doorway.*)

MAYA: It's too cold out here . . .

ADRIAN (*shuts the door to the room, draws her away from it*): For old times' sake . . .

MAYA: We'll talk tomorrow.

ADRIAN (*with a wild smile, excited eyes*): You're a government agent?

MAYA: What can I say? Will you believe anything?

ADRIAN (*on the verge of laughter*): My spine is tingling. In my book, Maya—I may as well tell you, I've been struggling with my sanity the last ten minutes—in my book I made you an agent who screws all the writers and blackmails them so they'll give up fighting the government. And I abandoned it because I finally decided it was too melodramatic, the characters got lost in the plot. I invented it and I didn't believe it; and I'm standing here looking at you and *I still don't believe it!*

MAYA: Why should you?

ADRIAN (*instantly, pointing into her face*): That's what you say in the book! (*He grasps her hand passionately in both of his.*) Maya, listen—you've got to help me. I believe in your goodness. I don't care what you've done, I still believe that deep inside you're a rebel and you hate this goddamned government. You've got to tell me—I'll stay through the week—we'll talk, and you're going to tell me what goes on in your body, in your head, in this situation.

MAYA: Wait a minute . . .

ADRIAN (*kissing her hands*): Maya, you've made me believe in my book!

> *She suddenly turns her head. So does he. Then he sees her apprehension.*

You expecting somebody?

> *Voices are heard now from below. She is listening.*

Maya?

MAYA (*mystified*): Perhaps some friends of Marcus.

ADRIAN: He gives out the key?

MAYA: Go, please. Goodnight.

> *She enters the room. He follows her in.*

ADRIAN: You need any help?

> *A man and woman appear from upstage darkness in the corridor.*

MAYA: No—no, I am not afraid . . . (*She moves him to the door.*)

ADRIAN: I'll be glad to stay . . . (*He turns, sees the man, who is just approaching the door, a valise in his hand, wearing a raincoat.*) For Christ's sake—it's Marcus!

> MARCUS *is older, fifty-eight. He puts down his valise, spreads out his arms.*

MARCUS: Adrian!

> *Laughter. A girl, beautiful, very young, stands a step behind him as he and* ADRIAN *embrace.*

MAYA (*within the room*): Marcus?

MARCUS (*entering the room*): You're here, Maya! This is marvelous.

> *He gives her a peck. The girl enters, stands there looking around. He turns to* ADRIAN.

A friend of yours is parking my car. He'll be delighted to see you.

ADRIAN: Friend of *mine*?

MARCUS: Sigmund.

MAYA: Sigmund?

ADRIAN: Sigmund's *here*?

MARCUS: He's coming up for a drink. We ran into each other at the airport. (*To* MAYA:) Is there food? (*To* ADRIAN:) You'll stay, won't you? I'll call some people, we can have a party.

ADRIAN: Party? (*Flustered, he glances at* MAYA.) Well . . . yeah, great!

> *An understanding outburst of laughter between him and* MARCUS.

MAYA: There's only some ham. I'm going home. (*She turns to go upstage to the bedroom.*)

MARCUS (*instantly*): Oh, no, Maya! You mustn't. I was going to call you first thing . . . (*Recalling:*) Wait, I have something for you. (*He hurriedly zips open a pocket of his valise, takes out a pair of shoes in tissue.*) I had an hour in Frankfurt. Look, dear . . .

> *He unwraps the tissue. Her face lights. She half unwillingly takes them.*

MAYA: Oh, my God.

> MARCUS *laughs. She kicks off a shoe and tries one on.*

MARCUS: Right size?

IRINA (*as* MAYA *puts on the other shoe*): Highly beautiful.

> MAYA *takes a few steps, watching her feet, then goes to* MARCUS *and gives him a kiss, then looks into his eyes with a faint smile, her longing and hatred.*

MARCUS (*taking out folds of money*): Here, darling . . . ask Mrs. Andrus to prepare something, will you? (*He hands her money.*) Let's have an evening. (*He starts her toward the bedroom door upstage—*) But come and put something on, it's raining. (*—and comes face to face with the girl.*) Oh, excuse me—this is Irina . . .

> MAYA *barely nods, and goes back to pick up her other shoes.*

ADRIAN: I'll go along with you, Maya— (*He reaches for his coat.*)

MARCUS: No, it's only down the street. Irina, this is my good friend Maya.

IRINA: 'Aloo.

> MAYA *silently shakes her hand.*

MARCUS: And here is Adrian Wallach. Very important American writer.

MAYA *exits upstage.*

ADRIAN: How do you do?

IRINA: 'Aloo. I see you Danemark.

ADRIAN: She's going to see me in Denmark?

MARCUS: She's Danish. But she speaks a little English.

IRINA (*with forefinger and thumb barely separated, to* ADRIAN): Very small.

ADRIAN: When do you want to meet in Denmark?

MAYA *enters putting on a raincoat.*

MAYA: Sausages?

MARCUS: And maybe some cheese and bread and some fruit. I'll open wine.

IRINA: I see your book.

ADRIAN (*suddenly, as* MAYA *goes for the door*): Wait! I'll walk her there . . .

MAYA *hesitates at the door.*

MARCUS (*grasping* ADRIAN'*s arm, laughing*): No, no, no, you are our guest; please, it's only two doors down. Maya doesn't mind.

MAYA *starts out to the door.* SIGMUND *appears in the corridor, a heavy man shaking out his raincoat. He is in his late forties. She halts before the doorway.*

MAYA (*questioningly, but with a unique respect*): Sigmund.

SIGMUND: Maya.

He kisses the palm of her hand. For a moment they stand facing each other.

MARCUS: Look who we have here, Sigmund!

MAYA *exits up the corridor as* SIGMUND *enters the room.*

SIGMUND: Oh—my friend! (*He embraces* ADRIAN, *laughing, patting his back.*)

ADRIAN: How's it going, Sigmund? (*He grasps Sigmund's hand.*) What a terrific surprise! How's your cold, did you take my pills?

SIGMUND: Yes, thank you. I take pills, vodka, brandy, whisky— now I have only headache. (*With a nod to* IRINA:) *Grüss Gott.*

MARCUS *goes and opens a chest, brings bottles and glasses to the marble table.*

IRINA: *Grüss Gott.*

ADRIAN: Oh, you speak German?

IRINA (*with the gesture*): Very small.

MARCUS: Come, help yourselves. (*He takes a key ring out of his valise.*) I have whisky for you, Adrian.

ADRIAN: I'll drink brandy. How about you, Sigmund?

SIGMUND: For me whisky.

MARCUS (*taking out an address book*): I'll call a couple of people, all right?

ADRIAN: *Girls!*

SIGMUND *sits downstage, takes out a cigarette.*

MARCUS: If you feel like it.

ADRIAN (*glancing at* SIGMUND, *who is lighting up*): Maybe better just us.

MARCUS: Sigmund likes a group. (*He picks up his valise.*)

SIGMUND: What you like.

ADRIAN (*to* MARCUS): Well, okay.

MARCUS (*pointing upstage to* IRINA): Loo?

IRINA: Oh, ja!

MARCUS (*holding* IRINA *by the waist and carrying the valise in his free hand as they move upstage; to* SIGMUND): We can talk in the bedroom in a little while. (*He exits with* IRINA.)

ADRIAN: That's a nice piece of Danish.

> SIGMUND *draws on his cigarette.* ADRIAN *gets beside him and taps his shoulder;* SIGMUND *turns up to him.* ADRIAN *points to ceiling, then to his own ear.*

Capeesh?

SIGMUND (*turns front, expressionless*): The police have confiscated my manuscript.

ADRIAN (*his hand flying out to grip Sigmund's shoulder*): No! Oh, Jesus—when?

SIGMUND: Now. Tonight.

ADRIAN (*glancing quickly around, to cover their conversation*): He had a record player . . .

SIGMUND (*with a contemptuous wave toward the ceiling*): No—I don't care.

ADRIAN: The last fifteen, twenty minutes, you mean?

SIGMUND: Tonight. They have take it away.

ADRIAN: My God, Sigmund . . .

> SIGMUND *turns to him.*

I mentioned something to Maya, but I had no idea it was really . . . (*He breaks off, pointing to the ceiling.*)

SIGMUND: When, you told Maya?

ADRIAN: In the last fifteen minutes or so.

SIGMUND: No—they came earlier—around six o'clock.

ADRIAN: Nearly stopped my heart . . .

SIGMUND: No, I believe they find out for different reason.

ADRIAN: Why?

SIGMUND: I was so happy.

> *Pause.*

ADRIAN: So they figured you'd finished the book?

SIGMUND: I think so. I worked five years on this novel.

ADRIAN: How would they know you were happy?

SIGMUND (*pause; with a certain projection*): In this city, a man my age who is happy, attract attention.

ADRIAN: . . . Listen. When I leave tomorrow you can give . . . (*He stops himself and glances upstage to the bedroom doorway, taking out a notebook and pencil. As he writes, speaking in a tone of forced relaxation:*) Before I leave you've got to give me a tour of the Old Roman bath . . .

> *He shows the page to* SIGMUND, *who reads it and looks up at him.* SIGMUND *shakes his head negatively.*

(*Horrified:*) They've got the only . . . ?

> SIGMUND *nods positively and turns away.*

(*Appalled:*) Sigmund—why?

SIGMUND: I thought would be safer with . . . (*He holds up a single finger.*)

> *Pause.* ADRIAN *keeps shaking his head.*

ADRIAN (*sotto*): What are you doing here?

SIGMUND: I met him in the airport by accident.

ADRIAN: What were you doing at the airport?

SIGMUND: To tell my wife. She works there.

ADRIAN: I thought she was a chemist.

SIGMUND: She is wife to me—they don't permit her to be chemist. She clean the floor, the windows in the airport.

ADRIAN: Oh, Jesus, Sigmund . . . (*Pause.*) Is there anything you can do?

SIGMUND: I try.

ADRIAN: Try what?

> SIGMUND *thumbs upstage.*

Could he?

> SIGMUND *throws up his chin—tremendous influence.*

Would he?

> SIGMUND *mimes holding a telephone to his mouth, then indicates the bedroom doorway.*

Really? To help?

SIGMUND: Is possible.

ADRIAN: Can you figure him out?

> SIGMUND *extends a hand and rocks it, an expression of uncertainty on his face.*

ADRIAN: And Maya?

SIGMUND (*for a moment makes no answer*): Woman is always complicated.

ADRIAN: You know that they . . . lie a lot.

SIGMUND: Yes. (*Slight pause. He looks now directly into Adrian's eyes.*) Sometimes not.

ADRIAN: You don't think it's time to seriously consider . . . (*He spreads his arms wide like a plane, lifting them forward in a takeoff, then points in a gesture of flight.*) What I mentioned at dinner?

> SIGMUND *emphatically shakes his head no while pointing downward—he'll remain here.*

When we leave here I'd like to discuss whether there's really any point in that anymore.

> SIGMUND *turns to him.*

I don't know if it was in your papers, but there's a hearing problem all over the world. Especially among the young. Rock music, traffic—modern life is too loud for the human ear—you understand me. The subtler sounds don't get through much anymore.

> SIGMUND *faces front, expressionless.*

On top of that there's a widespread tendency in New York, Paris, London, for people to concentrate almost exclusively on shopping.

SIGMUND: I have no illusion.

ADRIAN: I hope not—shopping and entertainment. Sigmund?

> SIGMUND *turns to him, and* ADRIAN *points into his face, then makes a wide gesture to take in the room, the situation.*

Not entertaining. Not on anybody's mind in those cities.

SIGMUND: I know.

ADRIAN: Boring.

SIGMUND: Yes.

ADRIAN: Same old thing. It's the wrong style.

SIGMUND: I know.

ADRIAN: I meant what I said last night; I'd be happy to support—
(*He points at* SIGMUND, *who glances at him.*) Until a connection
is made with a university. (*He points to himself.*) Guarantee that.

> SIGMUND *nods negatively and spreads both hands—he will
> stay here.*

We can talk about it later. I'm going to ask you why. I don't
understand the point anymore. Not after this.

SIGMUND: You would also if it was your country.

ADRIAN: I doubt it. I would protect my talent. I saw a movie once
where they bricked up a man in a wall.

> MARCUS *enters in a robe, opening a whisky bottle.*

MARCUS: A few friends may turn up. (*He sets the whisky bottle on
the marble table. To* ADRIAN:) Will you excuse us for a few
minutes? Sigmund? (*He indicates the bedroom.*)

SIGMUND: I have told him.

> MARCUS *turns to* ADRIAN *with a certain embarrassment.*

ADRIAN: They wouldn't destroy it, would they?

> MARCUS *seems suddenly put upon, and unable to answer.*

Do you know?

MARCUS (*with a gesture toward the bedroom; to* SIGMUND): Shall
we?

SIGMUND (*standing*): I would like Adrian to hear.

ADRIAN (*to* MARCUS): Unless you don't feel . . .

MARCUS (*unwillingly*): No—if he wishes, I have no objection.

SIGMUND *sits.*

ADRIAN: If there's anything I can do you'll tell me, will you?

MARCUS (*to* SIGMUND): Does Maya know?

SIGMUND: She was going out.

MARCUS (*as a muted hope for alliance*): I suppose she might as well. But it won't help her getting excited.

SIGMUND: She will be calm, Maya is not foolish.

ADRIAN: Maybe we ought to get into it, Marcus—they wouldn't destroy the book, would they?

MARCUS (*with a fragile laugh*): That's only one of several questions, Adrian—the first thing is to gather our thoughts. Let me get your drink. (*He stands.*)

ADRIAN: I can wait with the drink. Why don't we get into it?

MARCUS: All right. (*He sits again.*)

ADRIAN: Marcus?

   MARCUS *turns to him. He points to the ceiling.*

I know.

   MARCUS *removes his gaze from* ADRIAN, *a certain mixture of embarrassment and resentment in his face.*

Which doesn't mean I've drawn any conclusions about anyone. I mean that sincerely.

MARCUS: You understand, Adrian, that the scene here is not as uncomplicated as it may look from outside. You must believe me.

ADRIAN: I have no doubt about that, Marcus. But at the same time I wouldn't want to mislead you . . . (*he glances upward*) . . . or anyone else. If that book is destroyed or not returned to him—

for whatever it's worth I intend to publicize what I believe is an act of barbarism. This is not some kind of an issue for me—this man is my brother.

Slight pause. MARCUS *is motionless. Then he turns to* ADRIAN *and gestures to him to continue speaking, to amplify.* ADRIAN *looks astonished.* MARCUS *repeats the gesture even more imperatively.*

For example . . . I've always refused to peddle my books on television, but there's at least two national network shows would be glad to have me, and for this I'd go on.

He stops; MARCUS *gestures to continue.*

Just telling the story of this evening would be hot news from coast to coast—including Washington, D.C., where some congressmen could easily decide we shouldn't sign any more trade bills with this country. And so on and so forth.

MARCUS: It was brandy, wasn't it?

ADRIAN (*still amazed*): . . . Thanks, yes.

MARCUS *goes to get the drinks.* ADRIAN *catches Sigmund's eye, but the latter turns forward thoughtfully.* IRINA *enters, heading for the drinks.* MARCUS *brings* ADRIAN *a brandy as she makes herself a drink. In the continuing silence,* MARCUS *returns to the drink table, makes a whisky, and takes it down to* SIGMUND. ADRIAN *turns toward* IRINA, *upstage.*

So how's everything in Denmark?

IRINA (*with a pleasant laugh*): No, no, not everything.

ADRIAN (*thumbing to the ceiling, to* SIGMUND): *That* ought to keep them busy for a while.

MARCUS (*chuckles, sits with his own drink*): Cheers.

ADRIAN: Cheers.

SIGMUND: Cheers.

> *They drink.* IRINA *brings a drink, sits on the floor beside* MARCUS.

MARCUS: Have you been to London this time?

ADRIAN (*pauses slightly, then glances toward* SIGMUND): . . . No. How was London?

MARCUS: It's difficult there. It seems to be an endless strike.

ADRIAN (*waits a moment*): Yes. (*He decides to continue.*) Last time there my British publisher had emphysema and none of the elevators were working. I never heard so many Englishmen talking about a dictatorship before.

MARCUS: They probably have come to the end of it there. It's too bad, but why should evolution spare the English?

ADRIAN: Evolution toward what—fascism?

MARCUS: Or the Arabs taking over more of the economy.

ADRIAN: I can see the bubble pipes in the House of Commons.

> *Laughter.*

The Honorable Member from Damascus.

> *Laughter. It dies.* ADRIAN *thumbs toward* SIGMUND *and then to the ceiling, addressing* MARCUS.

If they decide to give an answer, would it be tonight?

MARCUS (*turns up his palms*): . . . Relax, Adrian. (*He drinks.*) Please.

ADRIAN (*swallows a glassful of brandy*): This stuff really spins the wheels. (*He inhales.*)

MARCUS: It comes from the mountains.

ADRIAN: I feel like I'm on one.

MARCUS: What's New York like now?

ADRIAN: New York? New York is another room in hell. (*He looks up.*) Of course not as architecturally ornate. In fact, a ceiling like this in New York—I can't imagine it lasting so long without some half-crocked writer climbing up and chopping holes in those cherubim.

MARCUS: The ceiling is nearly four hundred years old, you know.

ADRIAN: That makes it less frightful?

MARCUS: In a sense, maybe—for us it has some reassuring associations. When it was made, this city was the cultural capital of Europe—the world, really, this side of China. A lot of art, science, philosophy poured from this place.

ADRIAN: Painful.

MARCUS (*with a conceding shrug*): But on the other hand, the government spends a lot keeping these in repair. It doesn't do to forget that, you know.

SIGMUND: That is true. They are repairing all the angels. It is very good to be an angel in our country.

> MARCUS *smiles.*

Yes, we shall have the most perfect angels in the whole world.

> MARCUS *laughs.*

But I believe perhaps every government is loving very much the angels, no, Adrian?

ADRIAN: Oh, no doubt about it. But six months under this particular kind of art and I'd be ready to cut my throat or somebody else's. What do you say we go to a bar, Marcus?

MARCUS (*to* SIGMUND): *Ezlatchu stau?*

SIGMUND (*sighs, then nods*): *Ezlatchu.*

ADRIAN (*to* MARCUS): Where does that put us?

MARCUS: He doesn't mind staying till we've had something to eat. Afterwards, perhaps.

Pause. Silence.

ADRIAN: Let me in on it, Marcus—are we waiting for something?

MARCUS: No, no, I just thought we'd eat before we talked.

ADRIAN: Oh. All right.

IRINA (*patting her stomach*): I to sandwich?

MARCUS (*patting her head like a child's, laughing*): Maya is bringing very soon.

ADRIAN: She's as sweet as sugar, Marcus, where'd you find her?

MARCUS: Her husband is the head of Danish programming for the BBC. *There's* MAYA. (*He crosses to the corridor door.*)

ADRIAN: What does he do, loan her out?

MARCUS (*laughs*): No, no, she just wanted to see the country. (*He exits into the corridor.*)

SIGMUND: And Marcus will show her every inch.

ADRIAN (*bursts out laughing*): Oh Sigmund, Sigmund—what a century! (*Sotto:*) What the hell is happening?

Men's shouting voices below, MAYA *yelling loudly.* MARCUS *instantly breaks into a run, disappears up the corridor.* ADRIAN *and* SIGMUND *listen. The shouting continues.* SIGMUND *gets up, goes and listens at the door.*

ADRIAN: What is it?

SIGMUND opens the door, goes into the corridor, listens.

Who are they?

A door is heard slamming below, silencing the shouts. Pause.

Sigmund?

SIGMUND *comes back into the room.*

What was it?

SIGMUND: Drunken men. They want to see the traitor to the motherland. Enemy of the working class. (*He sits.*)

Pause.

ADRIAN: . . . Come to my hotel.

SIGMUND: Is not possible. Be calm.

ADRIAN: How'd they know you were here?

SIGMUND *shrugs, then indicates the ceiling.*

They'd call out hoodlums?

SIGMUND *turns up his palms, shrugs.*

MARCUS *and* MAYA *appear up the corridor. She carries a large tray covered with a white cloth. He has a handkerchief to his cheekbone. He opens the door for her.* IRINA *stands and clears the marble table for the tray.* MARCUS *crosses to the upstage right doorway and exits.*

SIGMUND *stands.* MAYA *faces him across the room. Long pause.*

What happened?

MAYA (*with a gesture toward the food*): Come, poet.

SIGMUND *watches her for a moment more, then goes up to the food. She is staring excitedly into his face.*

The dark meat is goose.

SIGMUND *turns from her to the food.*

Adrian?

ADRIAN: I'm not hungry. Thanks.

MAYA (*takes the plate from* SIGMUND *and loads it heavily*): Beer?

SIGMUND: I have whisky. You changed your haircut?

MAYA: From *Vogue* magazine. You like it?

SIGMUND: Very.

MAYA (*touching his face*): Very much, you say.

SIGMUND: Very, very much.

> *He returns to his chair with a loaded plate, sits, and proceeds to eat in silence. She pours herself a brandy, sits near him.*

MAYA (*to* ADRIAN *as she watches* SIGMUND *admiringly*): He comes from the peasants, you know. That is why he is so beautiful. And he is sly. Like a snake.

> *Slight pause.* SIGMUND *eats.*

What have you done now? (*She indicates below.*) Why have they come?

> SIGMUND *pauses in his eating, not looking at her.*

ADRIAN (*after the pause*): The cops took his manuscript tonight.

> *She inhales sharply with a gasp, nearly crying out.* SIGMUND *continues to eat. She goes to him, embraces his head, mouth pressed to his hair. He draws her hands down, apparently warding off her emotion, and continues eating. She moves and sits further away from him, staring ahead, alarmed and angry.* MARCUS *enters from the bedroom, a bandage stuck to his cheekbone.*

MARCUS (*to* ADRIAN): Have you taken something?

ADRIAN: Not just yet, thanks.

> MAYA *rises to confront* MARCUS, *but refusing her look, he passes her, a fixed smile on his face, picks up his drink from the marble table, and comes downstage and stands. First he,*

then ADRIAN, *then* MAYA, *turn and watch* SIGMUND *eating. He eats thoroughly.* IRINA *is also eating, off by herself.*

Pause.

MARCUS *goes to his chair, sits, and lights a cigarette.* ADRIAN *watches him.*

It's like some kind of continuous crime.

MAYA: You are so rich, Adrian, so famous—why do you make such boring remarks?

ADRIAN: Because I am a bore.

MARCUS: Oh, now, Maya . . .

MAYA (*sharply, to* MARCUS): Where is it not a continuous crime?

SIGMUND: It is the truth. (*To* ADRIAN:) Just so, yes. It is a continuous crime.

MAYA (*to the three*): Stupid. Like children. Stupid!

MARCUS: *Sssh*—take something to eat, dear . . .

ADRIAN: Why are we stupid?

Ignoring his question, she goes up to the table, takes a goose wing, and bites into it. Then she comes down and stands eating. After a moment . . .

MARCUS: It's wonderful to see you again, Adrian. What brought you back?

MAYA: He has been talking to Allison Wolfe.

MARCUS (*smiling, to* ADRIAN): Oh, to Allison.

ADRIAN: Yes.

MARCUS: Is he still going around with that story?

MAYA: Yes.

MARCUS (*slight pause*): Adrian . . . you know, I'm sure, that this house has been a sort of gathering place for writers for many years now. And they've always brought their girlfriends, and quite often met girls here they didn't know before. Our first literary magazine after the war was practically published from this room.

ADRIAN: I know that, Marcus.

MARCUS: Allison happened to be here one night, a month or so ago, when there was a good bit of screwing going on.

ADRIAN: Sorry I missed it.

MARCUS: It *was* fairly spectacular. But believe me—it was a purely spontaneous outburst of good spirits. Totally unexpected, it was just one of those things that happens with enough brandy.

ADRIAN *laughs.*

What I think happened is that—you see, we had a novelist here who was about to emigrate; to put it bluntly, he is paranoid. I can't blame him—he hasn't been able to publish here since the government changed. And I am one of the people he blamed, as though I had anything to say about who is or isn't to be published. But the fact that I live decently and can travel proved to him that I have some secret power with the higher echelons—in effect, that I am some sort of agent.

ADRIAN: Those are understandable suspicions, Marcus.

MARCUS (*with a light laugh*): But why!

MAYA: It is marvelous, Adrian, how understandable everything is for you.

ADRIAN: I didn't say that at all, Maya; I know practically nothing about Marcus, so I could hardly be making an accusation, could I?

MARCUS: Of course not. It's only that the whole idea is so appalling.

ADRIAN: Well, I apologize. But it's so underwater here an outsider is bound to imagine all sorts of nightmares.

MAYA: You have no nightmares in America?

ADRIAN: You know me better than that, Maya—of course we have them, but they're different.

IRINA (*revolving her finger*): Is music?

MARCUS: In a moment, dear.

MAYA: I really must say, Adrian—when you came here the other times it was the Vietnam War, I believe. Did anyone in this country blame you personally for it?

ADRIAN: No, they didn't. But it's not the same thing, Maya.

MAYA: It never is, is it?

ADRIAN: I was arrested twice for protesting the war. Not that that means too much—we had lawyers to defend us, and the networks had it all over the country the next day. So there's no comparison, and maybe I know it better than most people. And that's why I'm not interested in blaming anyone here. This is impossible, Marcus, why don't we find a restaurant, I'm beginning to sound like an idiot.

MARCUS: We can't now, I've invited . . .

ADRIAN: Then why don't you meet us somewhere. Sigmund? What do you say, Maya—where's a good place?

MARCUS: Not tonight, Adrian.

> ADRIAN *turns to him, catching a certain obscure decision.* MARCUS *addresses* SIGMUND.

I took the liberty of asking Alexandra to stop by.

> SIGMUND *turns his head to him, surprised.* MAYA *turns to* MARCUS *from upstage, the plate in her hand.*

(*To* MAYA:) I thought he ought to talk to her. (*To* SIGMUND:) I hope you won't mind.

MAYA (*turns to* SIGMUND, *with a certain surprise*): You will talk with Alexandra?

SIGMUND *is silent.*

IRINA (*revolving her finger*): Jazz?

MARCUS: In a moment, dear.

SIGMUND: She is coming?

MARCUS: She said she'd try. I think she will. (*To* ADRIAN:) She is a great admirer of Sigmund's.

MAYA *comes down to* ADRIAN *with a plate. She is watching* SIGMUND, *who is facing front.*

MAYA: I think you should have asked if he agrees.

MARCUS: I don't see the harm. She can just join us for a drink, if nothing more.

ADRIAN (*accepting the plate*): Thanks. She a writer?

MAYA: Her father is the Minister of Interior. (*She points at the ceiling.*) He is in charge . . .

ADRIAN: Oh! I see. (*He turns to watch* SIGMUND, *who is facing front.*)

MARCUS: She writes poetry.

MAYA: Yes. (*She glances anxiously to* SIGMUND.) Tremendous . . . (*spreads her arms*) . . . *long* poems. (*She takes a glass and drinks deeply.*)

MARCUS (*on the verge of sharpness*): Nevertheless, I think she has a certain talent.

MAYA: Yes. You think she has a certain talent, Sigmund?

MARCUS: Now, Maya . . . (*He reaches out and lifts the glass from her hand.*)

MAYA: Each year, you see, Adrian—since her father was appointed, this woman's poetry is more and more admired by more and more of our writers. A few years ago only a handful appreciated her, but now practically everybody calls her a master. (*Proudly:*) Excepting for Sigmund—until now, anyway. (*She takes the glass from where* MARCUS *placed it.*)

SIGMUND (*pause*): She is not to my taste . . . (*he hesitates*) . . . but perhaps she is a good poet.

MAYA (*slight pause*): But she has very thick legs.

    MARCUS *turns to her.*

But that must be said, Marcus . . . (*She laughs.*) We are not yet obliged to overlook a fact of nature. Please say she has thick legs.

MARCUS: I have no interest in her legs.

MAYA: Sigmund, my darling—surely you will say she . . .

MARCUS: Stop that, Maya . . .

MAYA (*suddenly, at the top of her voice*): It is important! (*She turns to* SIGMUND.)

SIGMUND: She has thick legs, yes.

MAYA: Yes. (*She presses his head to her hip.*) Some truths will not change, and certain people, for all our sakes, are appointed never to forget them. How do the Jews say?—If I forget thee, O Jerusalem, may I cut off my hand? . . . (*To* IRINA:) You want jazz?

IRINA (*starts to rise, happily*): Jazz!

MAYA (*helping her up*): Come, you poor girl, we have hundreds

. . . I mean he does. (*She laughs.*) My God, Marcus, how long I lived here. (*She laughs, nearly weeping.*) I'm going crazy . . .

SIGMUND (*stands*): I must walk. I have eaten too much. (*He buttons his jacket.*)

ADRIAN (*indicating below*): What about those men?

> SIGMUND *beckons* ADRIAN *toward the double doors at left. He moves toward the left door, which he opens as* ADRIAN *stands, starts after him, then halts and turns with uncertainty to* MARCUS *and* MAYA, *who look on without expression.* ADRIAN *goes out, shutting the door.* SIGMUND *is standing in the corridor.*

MAYA (*to* IRINA): Come, we have everything. (*She goes and opens an overhead cabinet, revealing hundreds of records.*) From Paris, London, New York, Rio . . . you like conga?

> IRINA *reads the labels.* MAYA *turns her head toward the corridor.* MARCUS *now turns as well.*

SIGMUND: Do you understand?

ADRIAN: No.

SIGMUND: I am to be arrested.

ADRIAN: How do you know that?

SIGMUND: Alexandra is the daughter of . . .

ADRIAN: I know—the Minister of . . .

SIGMUND: Marcus would never imagine I would meet with this woman otherwise.

ADRIAN: Why? What's she about?

SIGMUND: She is collecting the dead for her father. She arrange for writers to go before the television and apologize to the government. *Mea culpa*—to kissing their ass.

Slight pause.

ADRIAN: I think you've got to leave the country, Sigmund.

MAYA crosses the room.

SIGMUND: Is impossible. We cannot discuss it.

MAYA enters the corridor, closing the door behind her.

MAYA: Get out.

SIGMUND (*comes to her, takes her hand gently*): I must talk to Adrian.

MAYA: Get out, get out! (*To* ADRIAN:) He must leave the country. (*To* SIGMUND:) Finish with it! Tell Marcus.

SIGMUND (*turns her to the door, a hand on her back, and opens the door for her*): Please, Maya.

She enters the room, glancing back at him in terror. He shuts the door.

IRINA (*holding out a record*): Play?

MAYA looks to MARCUS, who turns away. Then she goes and uncovers a record player, turns it on, sets the record on it. During the following the music plays, a jazz piece or conga. First IRINA dances by herself, then gets MARCUS up and dances with him. MAYA sits, drinking.

Pause.

SIGMUND: You have a pistol?

ADRIAN: . . . A pistol?

SIGMUND: Yes.

ADRIAN: No. Of course not. (*Pause.*) How could I carry a pistol on an airplane?

SIGMUND: Why not? He has one in his valise. I saw it.

Pause.

ADRIAN: What good would a pistol do?

Pause.

SIGMUND: . . . It is very difficult to get pistol in this country.

ADRIAN: This is unreal, Sigmund, you can't be thinking of a . . .

SIGMUND: If you will engage him in conversation, I will excuse myself to the bathroom. He has put his valise in the bedroom. I will take it from the valise.

ADRIAN: And do what with it?

SIGMUND: I will keep it, and he will tell them that I have it. In this case they will not arrest me.

ADRIAN: But why not?

SIGMUND: They will avoid at the present time to shoot me.

ADRIAN: . . . And I'm to do . . . what am I to . . .

SIGMUND: It is nothing; you must only engage him when I am excusing myself to the bathroom. Come . . .

ADRIAN: Let me catch my breath, will you? . . . It's unreal to me, Sigmund, I can't believe you have to do this.

SIGMUND: It is not dangerous, believe me.

ADRIAN: Not for me, but I have a passport. . . . Then this is why Marcus came back?

SIGMUND: I don't know. He has many friend in the government, but . . . I don't know why.

ADRIAN: He's an agent.

SIGMUND: Is possible not.

ADRIAN: Then what is he?

SIGMUND: Marcus is Marcus.

ADRIAN: Please, explain to me. I've got to understand before I go in there.

SIGMUND: It is very complicated between us.

ADRIAN: Like what? Maya?

SIGMUND: Maya also. (*Slight pause.*) When I was young writer, Marcus was the most famous novelist in our country. In Stalin time he has six years in prison. He cannot write. I was not in prison. When he has returned I am very popular, but he was forgotten. It is tragic story.

ADRIAN: You mean he's envious of you.

SIGMUND: This is natural.

ADRIAN: But didn't you say he's protected you . . .

SIGMUND: Yes, of course. Marcus is very complicated man.

ADRIAN: But with all that influence, why can't you sit down and maybe he can think of something for you.

SIGMUND: He has thought of something—he has thought of Alexandra.

ADRIAN: You mean he's trying to destroy you.

SIGMUND: No. Is possible he believes he is trying to help me.

ADRIAN: But subconsciously . . .

SIGMUND: Yes. Come, we must go back.

ADRIAN: Just one more minute. You're convinced he's not an agent.

SIGMUND: My opinion, no.

ADRIAN: But how does he get all these privileges?

SIGMUND: Marcus is lazy. Likewise, he is speaking French, English, German—five, six language. When the foreign writers are coming, he is very gentleman, he makes amusing salon, he is showing the castles, the restaurants, introduce beautiful girls. When these writers return home they say is no bad problem in this civilized country. He makes very nice impression, and for this they permit him to be lazy. Is not necessary to be agent.

ADRIAN: You don't think it's possible that he learned they were going to arrest you and came back to help you?

SIGMUND *looks at him, surprised.*

That makes as much sense as anything else, Sigmund. Could he have simply wanted to do something decent? Maybe I'm being naive, but if he wanted your back broken, his best bet would be just to sit tight in London and let it happen.

SIGMUND *is silent.*

And as for calling Alexandra—maybe he figured your only chance *is* actually to make peace with the government.

SIGMUND *is silent.*

You grab that gun and you foreclose everything—you're an outlaw. Is it really impossible to sit down with Marcus, man to man? I mean, you're pinning everything on an interpretation, aren't you?

SIGMUND: I know Marcus.

ADRIAN: Sigmund—every conversation I've ever had with him about this country, he's gone out of his way to praise you—your talent and you personally. I can't believe I was taken in; he genuinely admires your guts, your resistance. Let me call him out here.

SIGMUND *turns, uncertain but alarmed.*

What's to lose? Maybe there's a string he can pull, let's put *his* feet to the fire. Because he's all over Europe lamenting conditions here, he's a big liberal in Europe. I've seen him get girls with those lamentations. Let me call him on it.

SIGMUND (*with a blossoming suspicion in the corners of his eyes*): I will never make speech on the television . . .

ADRIAN (*alarmed*): For Christ's sake, Sigmund, you don't imagine *I* would want that. (*He explodes.*) This is a quagmire, a fucking asylum! . . . But I'm not helping out with any guns. It's suicide, you'll have to do that alone. (*He goes to the door.*)

SIGMUND: Adrian?

ADRIAN: I'm sorry, Sigmund, but that's the way I feel.

SIGMUND: I want my manuscript. If you wish to talk to Marcus, I have nothing to object . . . on this basis.

> ADRIAN *looks at him, unsatisfied, angry. He turns and flings the door open, enters the room.*

ADRIAN: Marcus? Can I see you a minute?

MARCUS: Of course. What is it?

ADRIAN: Out here, please . . . if you don't mind?

> MARCUS *crosses the room and enters the corridor.* SIGMUND *avoids Marcus's eyes, stands waiting.* MARCUS *turns to* ADRIAN *as he shuts the door.*

MARCUS: Yes?

> MAYA *opens the door, enters the corridor, shuts it behind her.* MARCUS *turns up his robe collar.*

ADRIAN (*breaks into an embarrassed grin*): I'm not sure what to say or not say. . . . I'm more of a stranger than I'd thought, Marcus . . .

MARCUS: We're all strangers in this situation—nobody ever learns how to deal with it.

ADRIAN: . . . I take it you have some contacts with the government.

MARCUS: Many of us do; it's a small country.

ADRIAN: I think they ought to know that, ah . . . (*He glances to* SIGMUND, *but* SIGMUND *is not facing in his direction.*) If he's to be arrested, he'll—resist.

> MAYA *turns quickly to* SIGMUND, *alarm in her face.*

MARCUS: I don't understand— (*To* SIGMUND, *with a faintly embarrassed grin:*) Why couldn't you have said that to me?

> SIGMUND, *bereft of an immediate answer, starts to turn to him.*

Well, it doesn't matter. (*He is flushed. He turns back to* ADRIAN.) Yes?

ADRIAN: What I thought was, that . . .

MARCUS: Of course, if we're talking about some—violent gesture, they will advertise it as the final proof he is insane. Which is what they've claimed all along. But what was your thought?

ADRIAN: I have the feeling that the inevitable is being accepted. They act and you react. I'd like to sit down, the four of us, and see if we can come up with some out that nobody's ever thought of before.

MARCUS: Certainly. But it's a waste of time if you think you can change their program.

ADRIAN: Which is what, exactly?

MARCUS: Obviously—to drive him out of the country. Failing that, to make it impossible for him to function.

ADRIAN: And you think?

MARCUS: There's no question in my mind—he must emigrate. They've taken the work of his last five years, what more do you want?

ADRIAN: There's no one at all you could approach?

MARCUS: With what? What can I offer that they need?

ADRIAN: Like what, for example?

MARCUS: Well, if he agreed to emigrate, conceivably they might let go of the manuscript—providing, of course, that it isn't too politically inflammatory. But that could be dealt with, I think—they badly want him gone.

ADRIAN: There's no one up there who could be made to understand that if they ignored him he would simply be another novelist . . .

MARCUS (*laughing lightly*): But will he ignore *them*? How is it possible? This whole country is inside his skin—that is his greatness—They have a right to be terrified.

ADRIAN: Supposing there were a copy of the manuscript.

MARCUS: But there isn't, so it's pointless talking about it.

ADRIAN: But if there were.

MARCUS: It might have been a consideration.

ADRIAN: . . . If they knew it would be published abroad.

MARCUS: It might slow them down, yes. But they know Sigmund's personality.

ADRIAN: How do you mean?

MARCUS: He's not about to trust another person with his fate—it's a pity; they'd never have found it in this house in a hundred years. The cellar's endless, the gallery upstairs full of junk—to me, this is the saddest part of all. If it had made a splash abroad it might have held their hand for six months, perhaps longer. (*With a regretful glance at* SIGMUND:) But . . . so it goes. (*Pause. He blows on his hands.*) It's awfully cold out here, come inside . . . (*He starts for the door.*)

ADRIAN: There's a copy in Paris.

MAYA *and* SIGMUND *turn swiftly to him.*

MARCUS: . . . In Paris.

ADRIAN: I sent it off this morning.

MARCUS: *This* morning?

ADRIAN: I ran into a cousin of mine; had no idea she was here. She took it with her to Gallimard—they're my publishers.

A broken smile emerges on Marcus's face. He is filling with a swirl of colors, glancing first at MAYA, *then at* SIGMUND, *then back to* ADRIAN.

MARCUS: Well, then . . . that much is solved. (*He goes to the door.*)

ADRIAN: They should be told, don't you think?

MARCUS (*stands at the door, his hand on the knob, finally turns to all of them*): How terrible. (*Slight pause. To* MAYA *and* SIGMUND:) *Such* contempt. (*Slight pause.*) Why? . . . Can you tell me? (*They avoid his gaze. He turns to* ADRIAN.) There's no plane to Paris today. Monday, Wednesday, and Friday. This is Tuesday, Adrian.

SIGMUND: I did not ask him to say that.

MARCUS: But perfectly willing to stand there and hope I'd believe it.

ADRIAN: I'm sorry, Marcus . . .

MARCUS (*laughing*): But Adrian, I couldn't care less.

MAYA (*moving to him*): Help him.

MARCUS: Absolutely not. I am finished with it. No one will ever manipulate me, I will not be in that position.

MAYA: He is a stupid man, he understands nothing!

ADRIAN: Now, hold it a second . . .

MAYA: Get out of here!

ADRIAN: Just hold it a second, goddammit! I'm out of my depth, Marcus, but I've apologized. I'm sorry. But you have to believe it was solely my invention; Sigmund has absolute faith in you.

SIGMUND: You can forgive him, Marcus—he tells you the truth; he believes you are my friend, he said this to me a moment ago.

ADRIAN: I feel he's drowning, Marcus, it was just something to grab for. (*He holds out his hand.*) Forgive me, it just popped out of my mouth.

MARCUS (*silently clasps his hand for an instant, and lets go; to* SIGMUND *and* MAYA *especially*): Come inside. We'll talk.

ADRIAN (*as* MARCUS *turns to the door*): . . . Marcus?

> MARCUS *turns to him. He is barely able to continue.*

Don't you think—it would be wiser—a bar or something?

MARCUS: I'm expecting Alexandra.

ADRIAN: Could you leave a note on the door? But it's up to you and Sigmund. (*To* SIGMUND:) What do you think?

SIGMUND (*hesitates*): It is for Marcus to decide. (*He looks at* MARCUS.) It is his house.

> MARCUS, *expressionless, stands silent.*

MAYA: Darling . . . (*delicately*) . . . it will endure a thousand years. (MARCUS *looks at her.*) . . . I've read it. It is all we ever lived. They must not, must not touch it. Whatever humiliation, whatever is necessary for this book, yes. More than he himself, more than any human being—this book they cannot harm. . . . Francesco's is still open. (*She turns to* ADRIAN.) But I must say to you, Adrian—nothing has ever been found in this house. We have looked everywhere.

ADRIAN: It's entirely up to Marcus. (*To* MARCUS:) You feel it's all right to talk in there?

Long pause.

MARCUS (*with resentment*): I think Maya has answered that question, don't you?

ADRIAN: Okay. Then you're not sure.

MARCUS: But you are, apparently.

ADRIAN (*slight pause; to* SIGMUND): I think I ought to leave.

SIGMUND: No, no . . .

ADRIAN: I think I'm only complicating it for you—

SIGMUND: I insist you stay . . .

ADRIAN (*laughs nervously, his arm touching Sigmund's shoulder*): I'm underwater, kid, I can't operate when I'm drowning. (*Without pausing, to* MARCUS:) I don't understand why you're offended.

MARCUS: The question has been answered once. There has never been any proof of an installation. But when so many writers congregate here, I've had to assume there might be something. The fact is, I have always warned people to be careful what they say in there—but only to be on the safe side. Is that enough?

SIGMUND: Come! (*To* MARCUS, *heartily, as he begins to press* ADRIAN *toward the door:*) Now I will have one big whisky . . .

MARCUS *laughs, starting for the door.*

ADRIAN (*separating himself from* SIGMUND): I'll see you tomorrow, Sigmund.

Silence. They go still.

This is all your marbles, kid. It's too important for anyone to be standing on his dignity. I think I'm missing some of the over-

tones. (*To* MARCUS:) But all I know is that if it were me I'd feel a
lot better if I could hear you say what you just said—in there.

MARCUS: What *I* said?

ADRIAN (*slight pause*): That you've always warned people that the
government might be listening, in that room.

SIGMUND: Is not necessary . . .

ADRIAN: I think it . . .

SIGMUND: Absolutely not! Please . . . (*He presses* ADRIAN *toward
the door and stretches his hand out to* MARCUS.) Come, Marcus,
please.

> SIGMUND *leads the way into the room, followed by* ADRIAN,
> *then* MARCUS *and* MAYA. *For an instant they are all awk-
> wardly standing there. Then* SIGMUND *presses his hand
> against his stomach.*

Excuse me one moment. (*He goes up toward the bedroom
doorway.*)

ADRIAN (*suddenly alerted, starts after* SIGMUND): Sigmund . . .

> But SIGMUND *is gone.* ADRIAN *is openly conflicted about
> rushing after him . . .*

MAYA: What is it?

ADRIAN (*blurting, in body-shock*): Level with him. Marcus . . .
this is your Hemingway, your Faulkner, for Christ's sake—
help him!

> SIGMUND *enters from bedroom, a pistol in his hand.* IRINA,
> *seeing it, strides away from him in fright.*

SIGMUND (*to* MARCUS): Forgive me. I must have it. (*He puts it in
his pocket.*)

IRINA (*pointing at his pocket*): Shoot?

SIGMUND: No, no. We are all friend. *Alle gute Freunde hier.*

IRINA: Ah. (*She turns questioningly to* MARCUS, *then* ADRIAN, MAYA, *and* SIGMUND.)

Pause.

ADRIAN: Marcus?

MARCUS, *at center, turns front, anger mounting in his face.* MAYA *goes and shuts off the record player. Then she turns to him, waiting.*

Will you say it? In here? Please?

END OF ACT ONE

Positions the same. A tableau, MARCUS at center, all waiting for him to speak. Finally he moves, glances at SIGMUND.

MARCUS: They are preparing a trial for you.

MAYA (*clapping her hands together, crying out*): Marcus!

> *She starts toward him, but he walks from her, turning away in impatience. She halts.*

When?

> MARCUS *is silent, downing his resentment.*

Do you know when?

MARCUS: I think within the month.

MAYA (*turning to* SIGMUND): My God, my God.

SIGMUND (*after a moment*): And Otto and Peter?

MARCUS: I don't know about them. (*He goes in the silence to his chair, sits.*)

> *Pause.*

ADRIAN: What would they charge him with?

MARCUS: . . . Fantastic. Break off a trip, fly across Europe, and now I'm asked—what am I asked?—to justify myself? Is that it?

> *Unable to answer,* ADRIAN *evades his eyes, then glances to* SIGMUND *for aid; but* SIGMUND *is facing front and now walks to a chair and sits.*

MAYA (*to* MARCUS): No, no, dear . . . (*Of* SIGMUND:) It's a shock for him . . .

61

MARCUS (*rejecting her apology, glances at* ADRIAN): . . . Section Nineteen, I'd imagine. Slandering the state.

ADRIAN: On what grounds?

MARCUS: He's been sending out some devastating letters to the European press; this last one to the United Nations—have you read that?

ADRIAN: Just now in Paris, yes.

MARCUS: What'd you think of it?

ADRIAN (*with a cautious glance at* SIGMUND): It was pretty hot, I guess— What's the penalty for that?

MARCUS: A year. Two, three, five—who knows?

Slight pause.

MAYA: It was good of you to return, dear.

MARCUS *does not respond. She invites Sigmund's gratitude.*

. . . Sigmund?

SIGMUND (*waits an instant*): Yes. Thank you, Marcus.

MARCUS *remains looking front.*

It is definite?

MARCUS: I think it is. And it will affect every writer in the country, if it's allowed to happen.

SIGMUND: How do you know this?

Slight pause.

MARCUS: My publisher had a press reception for me day before yesterday—for my book. A fellow from our London embassy turned up. We chatted for a moment, then I forgot about him, but in the street afterwards, he was suddenly beside me . . . we shared a cab. (*Slight pause. He turns directly to* SIGMUND.) He said he was from the Embassy Press Section.

SIGMUND: Police.

MARCUS (*lowers his eyes in admission*): He was . . . quite violent . . . his way of speaking.

SIGMUND: About me.

> *Slight pause.*

MARCUS: I haven't heard that kind of language . . . since . . . the old days. "You are making a mistake," he said, "if you think we need tolerate this scum any longer . . ."

MAYA: My God, my God . . .

MARCUS: "You can do your friend a favor," he said, "and tell him to get out this month or he will eat his own shit for five or six years."

> MAYA *weeps.*

"And as far as a protest in the West, he can wrap it in bacon fat and shove it up his ass." Pounded the seat with his fist. Bloodshot eyes. I thought he was going to hit me for a moment there. . . . It was quite an act.

ADRIAN: An act?

MARCUS: Well, he wasn't speaking for himself, of course. (*Slight pause.*) I started a letter, but I know your feelings about leaving—I felt we had to talk about it face to face.

SIGMUND: Please.

MARCUS (*hesitates, then turns to* ADRIAN): Are you here as a journalist?

ADRIAN: God, no—I just thought I'd stop by . . .

MAYA: He has written a novel about us.

MARCUS (*unguarded*): About us? Really! . . .

ADRIAN: Well, not literally . . .

MARCUS: When is it coming out?

ADRIAN: It won't. I've abandoned it.

MARCUS: Oh! That's too bad. Why?

ADRIAN: I'm not here to write about you, Marcus . . . honestly.

> MARCUS *nods, unconvinced.* ADRIAN *addresses* SIGMUND *as well.*

I'll leave now if you think I'm in the way . . .

> SIGMUND *doesn't react.*

MARCUS: It's all right. (*Slight pause.*) But if you decide to write something about us . . .

ADRIAN: I've no intention . . .

MARCUS (*smiling*): You never know. We have a tactical disagreement, Sigmund and I. To me, it's really a question of having had different experiences—although there are only seven or eight years between us; things that he finds intolerable are actually— from another viewpoint—improvements over the past . . .

ADRIAN (*indicating* MAYA): I only found out today you were in prison . . .

MARCUS: A camp, actually—we dug coal.

ADRIAN: Six years.

MARCUS: And four months.

ADRIAN: What for?

MARCUS: It's one of those stories which, although long, is not interesting. (*He laughs.*) The point is simple, in any case. We happen to occupy a . . . strategic zone, really—between two hostile ways of life. And no government here is free to do what it would like to do. But some intelligent, sympathetic people are up there now who weren't around in the old times, and to challenge these people, to even insult them, is to indulge in a sort of fantasy . . .

SIGMUND (*pointing to the ceiling*): Marcus, this is reality?

MARCUS: Let me finish . . .

SIGMUND: But is very important—who is fantastic? (*He laughs.*) We are some sort of characters in a poem which they are writing; is not my poem, is their poem . . . and I do not like this poem, it makes me crazy! (*He laughs.*)

ADRIAN: I understand what he means, though . . .

SIGMUND: I not! I am sorry. Excuse me, Marcus—please continue.

MARCUS (*slight pause*): They ought not be forced into political trials again . . .

SIGMUND: *I* am forcing . . .?

MARCUS: May I finish? It will mean a commitment which they will have to carry through, willingly or not. And that can only mean turning out the lights for all of us, and for a long time to come. It mustn't be allowed to happen, Sigmund. And it need not happen. (*Slight pause.*) I think you have to get out. For all our sakes.

> With an ironic shake of his head, SIGMUND makes a long exhale.

MARCUS: . . . I've called Alexandra because I think you need a line of communication now. If only to stall things for a time, or whatever you . . .

SIGMUND (*toward* MAYA): I must now communicate with *Alexandra.*

MARCUS: She adores your work, whatever you think of her.

SIGMUND *gives him a sarcastic glance.*

This splendid isolation has to end, Sigmund—it was never real, and now it's impossible.

SIGMUND (*shakes his head*): I will wait for her. I may wait?

MARCUS: I certainly hope you will. (*Slight pause.*) I only ask you to keep in mind that this goes beyond your personal feelings about leaving . . .

SIGMUND: I have never acted for personal feelings.

MARCUS (*insistently*): You've been swept away now and then—that United Nations letter could change nothing except enrage them . . .

SIGMUND: I may not also be enraged?

MAYA: Don't argue about it, please . . .

SIGMUND (*smiling at her*): Perhaps is time we argue . . .

MAYA: Sigmund, we are all too old to be right! (*She picks up a glass.*)

MARCUS: Are you getting drunk?

MAYA: No, I am getting sorry. Is no one to be sorry? I am sorry for both of you. I am sorry for Socialism. I am sorry for Marx and Engels and Lenin— (*She shouts to the air.*) I am sorry! (*To* IRINA, *irritably:*) Don't be frightened. (*She pours a drink.*)

Pause.

ADRIAN: I'd like to take back what I asked you before, Marcus.

MARCUS: How can I know what is in this room? How ludicrous can you get?

ADRIAN: I agree. I wouldn't be willing to answer that question in my house either.

SIGMUND: But would not be necessary to ask such question in your house.

ADRIAN: Oh, don't kid yourself . . .

MARCUS: The FBI is everywhere . . .

ADRIAN: Not everywhere, but they get around. The difference with us is that it's illegal.

SIGMUND: *Vive la différence.*

MARCUS: Provided you catch them.

ADRIAN (*laughs*): Right. (*He catches* SIGMUND's *dissatisfaction with him.*) I'm not saying it's the same . . .

SIGMUND (*turns away from* ADRIAN *to* MAYA): Please, Maya, a whisky.

MAYA (*eagerly*): Yes! (*She goes up to the drink table. Silence. She pours a drink, brings it to* SIGMUND.)

ADRIAN: Did this woman say what time she . . .

MARCUS: She's at some embassy dinner. As soon as she can break away. Shouldn't be long. (*Slight pause. He indicates Sigmund's pocket.*) Give me that thing, will you?

SIGMUND *does not respond.*

ADRIAN: Go ahead, Sigmund.

SIGMUND: I . . . keep for few minutes. (*He drinks.*)

Pause.

ADRIAN: I'm exhausted. (*He hangs his head and shakes it.*)

MAYA: You drink too fast.

ADRIAN: No . . . it's the whole thing—it suddenly hit me. (*He squeezes his eyes.*) Mind if I lie down?

MARCUS (*gesturing toward the couch*): Of course.

> ADRIAN *goes to the couch.*

What's *your* feeling?

ADRIAN: He's got to get out, I've told him that. (*He lies down.*) They're doing great, what do they need literature for? It's a pain in the ass. (*He throws an arm over his eyes, sighs.*) Christ . . . it's unbelievable. An hour from the Sorbonne.

MAYA (*a long pause; she sits between* SIGMUND *and* MARCUS, *glancing uncomfortably from one to the other*): It was raining in London?

MARCUS: No, surprisingly warm. How's your tooth?

MAYA (*pointing to a front tooth, showing him*): They saved it.

MARCUS: Good. He painted the bathroom.

MAYA: Yes, he came, finally. I paid him. The rest of the money is in the desk.

MARCUS: Thanks, dear. Looks very nice.

> *Slight pause.*

MAYA (*leans her elbow on her knee, her chin on her fist, observes her leg, then glances at* MARCUS): My bird died on Sunday.

MARCUS: Really? Lulu?

MAYA: Yes. I finally found out, though—she was a male. (*To* SIGMUND:) And all these years I called him Lulu!

SIGMUND: I can give you one of my rabbits.

MAYA: Oh, my God, no rabbits. (*She sighs.*) No birds, no cats, no dogs . . . Nothing, nothing anymore. (*She drinks.*)

Pause.

ADRIAN (*from the couch*): You ever get mail from your program?

MAYA: Oh, very much. Mostly for recipes, sometimes I teach them to cook.

SIGMUND: She is very comical. She is marvelous actress.

ADRIAN: It's not a political . . .?

MAYA: No! It's too early in the morning. I hate politics . . . boring, boring, always the same. . . . You know something? You are both very handsome.

> SIGMUND *and* MARCUS *look at her and laugh softly.*

You too, Adrian. (*She looks at her glass.*) And this is wonderful whisky.

MARCUS: Not too much, dear.

MAYA: No, no. (*She gets up with her glass, moves toward the window at right.*) There was such a marvelous line—that English poet, what was his name? Very famous . . . you published him in the first or second issue, I think. . . . "The world . . ." (*She presses her forehead.* MARCUS *observes her, and she sees him.*) I'm not drunk, it's only so long ago. Oh, yes! "The world needs a wash and a week's rest."

ADRIAN: Auden.

MAYA: Auden, yes! A wash and week's rest—what a wonderful solution.

ADRIAN: Yeah—last one into the Ganges is a rotten egg.

> *They laugh.*

MARCUS: Every now and then you sound like Brooklyn.

ADRIAN: That's because I come from Philadelphia. How do you know about Brooklyn?

MARCUS: I was in the American army.

ADRIAN (*amazed, sits up*): How do you come to the American army?

MAYA: He was sergeant.

MARCUS: I enlisted in London—we had to get out when the Nazis came. I was translator and interpreter for General McBride, First Army Intelligence.

ADRIAN: Isn't that funny? Every once in a while you come into a kind of—focus, that's very familiar. I've never understood it.

MARCUS: I was in almost three years.

ADRIAN: Huh! (*He laughs.*) I don't know why I'm so glad to hear it . . .

MARCUS: Well, you can place me now—we all want that.

ADRIAN: I guess so. What'd she mean, that you published Auden?

MAYA: Marcus was the editor of the magazine, until they closed it.

ADRIAN (*toward* SIGMUND): I didn't know that.

SIGMUND: Very good editor—Marcus was first editor who accept to publish my story.

MAYA: If it had been in English—or even French or Spanish—our magazine would have been as famous as the *New Yorker*.

MARCUS (*modestly*): Well . . .

MAYA (*to* MARCUS): In my opinion it was better . . . (*To* ADRIAN:) But our language even God doesn't read. People would stand on line in the street downstairs, like for bread. People from factories, soldiers from the army, professors . . . It was like some sort of Bible, every week a new prophecy. Pity you missed it . . . It was like living on a ship—every morning there was a different island.

MARCUS (*to* SIGMUND, *with a gesture of communication*): Elizabeth didn't look well, is she all right?

SIGMUND: She was very angry tonight. She is sometimes foolish.

Slight pause.

MAYA: Could he live, in America?

ADRIAN: I'm sure he could. Universities'd be honored to have him.

SIGMUND: I am speaking English like six-years-old child.

ADRIAN: Faculty wives'll be overjoyed to correct you. You'd be a big hit—with all that hair.

SIGMUND (*laughs dryly*): You are not going to Algeria?

MARCUS: On Friday.

ADRIAN: What's in Algeria?

MARCUS: There's a writers' congress—they've asked me to go.

ADRIAN: Communist countries?

MARCUS: Yes. But it's a big one—Arabs, Africans, Latin Americans . . . the lot.

SIGMUND: The French?

MARCUS: Some French, yes—Italians too, I think.

ADRIAN: What do you do at those things?

MAYA (*admiringly*): He represents our country—he lies on the beach with a gin and tonic.

MARCUS (*laughs*): It's too cold for the beach now. (*To* ADRIAN:) They're basically ideological discussions.

SIGMUND: Boring, no?

MARCUS: Agony. But there are some interesting people sometimes.

SIGMUND: You can speak of us there?

> MARCUS *turns to him, silent, unable to answer.*

No?

MARCUS: We're not on the agenda.

MAYA: It's difficult, dear . . .

SIGMUND: But perhaps privately—to the Italian comrades?
. . . French? Perhaps they would be interested for my manuscript.

> MARCUS *nods positively but turns up his palms—he'll do*
> *what he can.*

(*With the slightest edge of sarcasm:*) You will see, perhaps. (*He
chucks his head, closes his eyes with his face stretched upward,
his hand tapping frustratedly on his chair arm, his foot beat-
ing.*) So-so-so-so.

MARCUS (*looking front*): The important thing . . . is to be useful.

SIGMUND (*flatly, without irony*): Yes, always. (*Slight pause.*)
Thank you, that you have returned for this, I am grateful.

MARCUS: Whatever you decide, it ought to be soon. Once they
move to prosecute . . .

SIGMUND: Yes. I have still some questions—we can take a walk
later, perhaps.

MARCUS: All right. I've told you all I know . . .

SIGMUND: . . . About ourselves.

MARCUS (*surprised*): Oh. All right.

> *Pause.*

MAYA: How handsome you all are! I must say . . .

> MARCUS *laughs, she persists.*

Really, it's unusual for writers. (*Suddenly, to* IRINA:) And she is so lovely . . . *Du bist sehr schön.*

IRINA: *Danke.*

MAYA (*to* MARCUS): Isn't she very young?

MARCUS (*shrugs*): We only met two days ago.

MAYA (*touching his hair*): How marvelous. You are like God, darling—you can always create new people. (*She laughs, and with sudden energy:*) Play something, Sigmund! . . . (*She goes to* SIGMUND *to get him up.*) Come . . .

SIGMUND: No, no, no . . .

MAYA (*suddenly bends and kisses the top of his head, her eyes filling with tears*): Don't keep that thing . . .

> *She reaches for his pocket; he takes her hand and pats it, looking up at her. She stares down at him.*

The day he walked in here for the first time . . . (*She glances at* MARCUS.) Do you remember? The snow was half a meter high on his hat—I thought he was a peasant selling potatoes, he bowed the snow all over my typewriter. (*She glances at* ADRIAN.) And he takes out this lump of paper—it was rolled up like a bomb. A story full of colors, like a painting; this boy from the beet fields—a writer! It was a miracle—such prose from a field of beets. That morning—for half an hour—I believed Socialism. For half an hour I . . .

MARCUS (*cutting her off*): What brings you back, Adrian? (*The telephone rings in the bedroom.*) Probably for you.

MAYA: For me? (*She goes toward the bedroom.*) I can't imagine . . . (*She exits.*)

ADRIAN: I don't really know why I came. There's always been something here that I . . .

IRINA (*getting up, pointing to the piano*): I may?

MARCUS: Certainly . . . please.

IRINA *sits at the piano.*

SIGMUND: I think you will write your book again.

ADRIAN: I doubt it—there's a kind of music here that escapes me. I really don't think I dig you people.

IRINA (*testing the piano, she runs a scale; it is badly out of tune, and she makes a face, turning to* MARCUS): Ach . . .

MARCUS (*apologizing*): I'm sorry, it's too old to be tuned anymore . . . but go ahead . . .

MAYA (*entering*): There's no one—they cut off.

SIGMUND *turns completely around to her, alerted.*

MAYA (*to him, reassuringly*): I'm sure they'll call back . . . it was an accident. Good! You play?

IRINA *launches into a fast "Bei Mir Bist Du Schön," the strings whining.*

MAYA: Marvelous! Jitterbug! (*She breaks into a jitterbug with her glass in one hand, lifting her skirt.*) Come on, Adrian! . . . (*She starts for* ADRIAN.)

IRINA (*stops playing and stands up, pushing her fingers into her ears*): Is too, too . . .

MAYA: No, play, play . . .

IRINA (*refusing, laughing, as she descends onto the carpet beside* MARCUS, *shutting her ears*): Please, please, please . . .

MARCUS (*patting* IRINA): I believe she's done concerts . . . serious music. (*He looks at his watch; then, to* SIGMUND:) You're not going outside with that thing, are you?

SIGMUND *glances at him.*

It's absurd.

MAYA: It must be the Americans—ever since they started building that hotel the phones keep ringing.

ADRIAN: What hotel?

MAYA: The Hilton . . . three blocks from here. It's disarranged the telephones.

MARCUS: I'd love to read your novel—do you have it with you?

ADRIAN: It's no good.

MARCUS: That's surprising—what's the problem?

ADRIAN (*sits up*): Well . . . I started out with a bizarre, exotic quality. People sort of embalmed in a society of amber. But the longer it got, the less unique it became. I finally wondered if the idea of unfreedom can be sustained in the mind.

MARCUS: You relied on that.

ADRIAN: Yes. But I had to keep injecting melodramatic reminders. The brain tires of unfreedom. It's like a bad back—you simply learn to avoid making certain movements . . . like . . . whatever's in this ceiling; or if nothing is; we still have to live, and talk, and the rest of it. I really thought I knew, but I saw that I didn't; it's been an education tonight. I'd love to ask you something, Marcus—why do you carry a gun?

MARCUS: I don't, normally. I was planning a trip into the mountains in Algeria—still pretty rough up there in places. (*He looks at his watch.*)

MAYA: He fought a battle in Mexico last year. In the Chiapas. Like a cowboy.

MARCUS: Not really—no one was hurt.

ADRIAN: What the hell do you go to those places for?

MARCUS: It interests me—where there is no law, people alone with their customs. I started out to be an anthropologist.

ADRIAN: What happened?

MARCUS: The Nazis, the war. You were too young, I guess.

ADRIAN: I was in the army in the fifties, but after Korea and before Vietnam.

MARCUS: You're a lucky generation, you missed everything.

ADRIAN: I wonder sometimes. History came at us like a rumor. We were never really there.

MARCUS: Is that why you come here?

ADRIAN: Might be part of it. We're always smelling the smoke, but we're never quite sure who the devil really is. Drives us nuts.

MARCUS: You don't like ambiguity.

ADRIAN: Oh, sure—providing it's clear. (*He laughs.*) Or maybe it's always clearer in somebody else's country.

MARCUS: I was just about to say—the first time I came to America—a few years after the war . . .

ADRIAN: . . . You're not an American citizen, are you?

MARCUS: Very nearly, but I had a little . . . ambiguity with your Immigration Department. (*He smiles.*)

ADRIAN: You came from the wrong country.

MARCUS: No—it was the right country when I boarded ship for New York. But the Communists took over here while I was on the high seas. A Mr. Donahue, Immigration Inspector, Port of New York, did not approve. He put me in a cage.

ADRIAN: Why!

MARCUS: Suspicion I was a Red agent. Actually, I'd come on an invitation to lecture at Syracuse University. I'd published my first two—or it may have been three novels in Paris by then. I phoned the university—from my cage—and they were appalled, but no one lifted a finger, of course, and I was shipped back to Europe. It was terribly unambiguous, Adrian—you were a fascist country, to me. I was wrong, of course, but so it appeared. Anyway, I decided to come home and have a look here—I stepped off the train directly into the arms of our police.

ADRIAN: As an American spy.

MARCUS (*laughs*): What else?

ADRIAN (*nodding*): I got ya, Marcus.

MARCUS: Yes. (*Slight pause.*) But it's better now.

ADRIAN *glances at* Sigmund.

It has been, anyway. But one has to be of the generation that can remember. Otherwise, it's as you say—a sort of rumor that has no reality—excepting for oneself.

SIGMUND *drinks deeply from his glass. Slight pause.*

ADRIAN (*stands, and from behind* SIGMUND *looks down at him for an instant*): She's sure to come, huh?

MARCUS: I'm sure she will.

ADRIAN (*strolls to the window at right, stretches his back and arms, looks out of the window*): It's starting to snow. (*Slight pause.*) God, it's a beautiful city. (*He lingers there for a moment, then walks, his hands thrust into his back pockets.*) What do you suppose would happen if I went to the Minister of the Interior tonight—if I lost my mind and knocked on his door and raised hell about this?

MARCUS *turns to him, eyebrows raised.*

I'm serious.

MARCUS: Well . . . what happened when you tried to reason with Johnson or Nixon during Vietnam?

ADRIAN: Right. But of course we could go into the streets, which you can't . . .

SIGMUND: Why not?

ADRIAN (*surprised*): With all their tanks here?

SIGMUND: Yes, even so. (*Pause.*) Is only a question of the fantasy. In this country we have not Las Vegas. The American knows very well is almost impossible to winning money from this slot machine. But he is enjoying to experience hope. He is paying for the hope. For us, is inconceivable. Before such a machine we would experience only despair. For this reason we do not go into the street.

ADRIAN: You're more realistic about power . . .

SIGMUND: This is mistake, Adrian, we are not realistic. We also believe we can escaping power—by telling lies. For this reason, I think you have difficulty to write about us. You cannot imagine how fantastically we lie.

MARCUS: I don't think we're any worse than others . . .

SIGMUND: Oh, certainly, yes—but perhaps is not exactly lying because we do not expect to deceive anyone; the professor lies to the student, the student to the professor—but each knows the other is lying. We must lie, it is our only freedom. To lie is our slot machine—we know we cannot win, but it gives us the feeling of hope. Is like a serious play which no one really believes, but the technique is admirable. Our country is now a theatre, where no one is permitted to walk out and everyone is obliged to applaud.

MARCUS: That is a marvelous description, Sigmund—of the whole world.

SIGMUND: No, I must object—when Adrian speaks to me it is always his personal opinion. But with us, is impossible to speaking so simply, we must always making theatre.

MARCUS: I've been as plain as I know how to be. What is it you don't believe?

SIGMUND (*laughs*): But that is the problem in the theatre—I believe everything but I am convinced of nothing.

MAYA: It's enough.

SIGMUND: Excuse me, Maya—for me is not enough; if I am waking up in New York one morning, I must have concrete reason, not fantastic reason.

MAYA: Darling, they've taken your book . . .

SIGMUND (*with sudden force*): But is my country—is this reason to leave my country!

MAYA: There are people who love you enough to want to keep you from prison. What is fantastic about that?

SIGMUND (*turns to* MARCUS, *with a smile*): You are loving me, Marcus?

MARCUS, *overwhelmed by resentment, turns to* SIGMUND, *silent.*

Then we have not this reason. (*Slight pause.*) Therefore . . . perhaps you have come back for different reason.

MARCUS: I came back to prevent a calamity, a disaster for all of us . . .

SIGMUND: Yes, but is also for them a calamity. If I am in prison the whole world will know they are gangster. This is not intelligent—my book are published in nine country. For them is also disaster.

MARCUS: So this fellow in London? These threats? They're not serious?

SIGMUND: I am sure they wish me to believe so, therefore is very serious.

MARCUS: You don't believe a word I've told you, do you? There was no man at all in London; that conversation never happened? There'll be no arrest? No trial?

SIGMUND (*pause*): I think not.

MARCUS: Then give me back my pistol.

    SIGMUND *does not move.* MARCUS *holds out his hand.*

Give it to me, you're in no danger; I've invented the whole thing.

    SIGMUND *is motionless.*

Are you simply a thief? Why are you keeping it?

    SIGMUND *is silent.*

MAYA: Marcus . . .

MARCUS: I insist he answer me . . . (*To* SIGMUND:) Why are you keeping that pistol? (*He laughs.*) But of course you know perfectly well I've told you the truth; it was just too good an opportunity to cover me with your contempt . . . in her eyes and (*pointing toward* ADRIAN) the eyes of the world.

ADRIAN: Now, Marcus, I had no intention . . .

MARCUS: Oh, come now, Adrian, he's been writing this story for you all evening! *New York Times* feature on Socialist decadence.

ADRIAN: Now, wait a minute . . .

MARCUS: But it's so obvious! . . .

ADRIAN: Wait a minute, will you? He has a right to be uneasy.

MARCUS: No more than I do, and for quite the same reason.

ADRIAN: Why!

MARCUS (*laughs*): To whom am *I* talking, Adrian—the *New York Times,* or your novel, or you?

ADRIAN: For Christ's sake, are you serious?

MARCUS (*laughs*): Why not? You may turn out to be as dangerous to me as he believes I am to him. Yes!

> ADRIAN *looks astonished.*

Why is it any more absurd? Especially after that last piece of yours, which, you'll pardon me, was stuffed with the most primitive misunderstandings of what it means to live in this country. You haven't a clue, Adrian—you'll forgive me, but I have to say that. So I'm entitled to a bit of uneasiness.

ADRIAN: Marcus, are you asking me to account for myself?

MARCUS: By no means, but why must I?

MAYA: Why don't we all go to the playground and swing with the other children?

MARCUS (*laughs*): Very good, yes.

MAYA (*to* ADRIAN): Why is he so complicated? They allow him this house to store his father's library. These books earn hard currency. To sell them he must have a passport.

MARCUS: Oh, he knows all that, dear—it's hopeless; when did the facts ever change a conviction? It doesn't matter. (*He looks at his watch.*)

ADRIAN: It does, though. It's a terrible thing. It's maddening.

MARCUS (*denigrating*): Well . . .

ADRIAN: It is, you know it is. Christ, you're such old friends, you're writers . . . I never understood the sadness in this country, but I swear, I think it's . . .

MARCUS: Oh, come off it, Adrian—what country isn't sad?

ADRIAN: I think you've accepted something.

MARCUS: And you haven't?

ADRIAN: Goddammit, Marcus, we can still speak for ourselves! And not for some . . . (*He breaks off.*)

MARCUS: Some what?

ADRIAN (*walks away*): . . . Well, never mind.

MARCUS: I've spoken for no one but myself here, Adrian. If there seems to be some . . . unspoken interest . . . well, there is, of course. I am interested in seeing that this country does not fall back into darkness. And if he must sacrifice something for that, I think he should. That's plain enough, isn't it?

ADRIAN: I guess the question is . . . how you feel about that yourself.

MARCUS (*laughs*): But I feel terribly about it. I think it's dreadful. I think there's no question he is our best living writer. Must I go on, or is that enough? (*Silence.*) What change can feelings make? It is a situation which I can tell you—*no one wants* . . . no one. If I flew into an orgasm of self-revelation here it might seem more candid, but it would change nothing . . . except possibly to multiply the confusion.

MAYA (*to* ADRIAN): I think you were saying the same thing before. . . . Tell him.

MARCUS: What?

ADRIAN: Whether it matters anymore, what anyone feels . . . about anything. Whether we're not just some sort of . . . filament that only lights up when it's plugged into whatever power there is.

MAYA: It's interesting.

MARCUS: I don't know—it seems rather childish. When was a man ever conceivable apart from society? Unless you're looking for the angel who wrote each of our blessed names in his book of gold. The collective giveth and the collective taketh away—beyond that . . . (*he looks to the ceiling*) . . . was never anything but a sentimental metaphor; a God which now is simply a form of art. Whose style may still move us, but there was never any mercy in that plaster. The only difference now, it seems to me, is that we've ceased to expect any.

ADRIAN: I know one reason I came. I know it's an awkward question, but—those tanks bivouacked out there in the countryside . . . do they figure at all in your minds?

MAYA: Do you write *every minute*?

ADRIAN: Well, do they? (*To* MARCUS:) Are they part of your lives at all?

MARCUS: I don't really know . . .

ADRIAN: Maya? It interests me.

MAYA: It's such a long time, now. And you don't see them unless you drive out there . . .

MARCUS: It's hard to say.

ADRIAN (*of* SIGMUND): Why do you suppose he can't stop thinking about them? I bet there isn't an hour a day when they don't cross his mind.

MAYA: Because he is a genius. When he enters the tram, the conductor refuses to accept his fare. In the grocery store they give him the best oranges. The usher bows in the theatre when she shows him to his seat. (*She goes to* SIGMUND, *touches his hair.*) He is our Sigmund. He is loved, he creates our memories. Therefore, it is only a question of time when he will create the departure of these tanks and they will go home. And then we shall all be ourselves, with nothing overhead but the sky, and he will turn into a monument standing in the park. (*Her eyes fill with tears, she turns up his face.*) Go, darling. Please. There is nothing left for you.

SIGMUND (*touches her face*): Something, perhaps. We shall see.

MAYA *moves right to the window, sips a drink.*

IRINA (*with a swimming gesture, to* MARCUS): I am bathing?

MARCUS: Yes, of course—come, I'll get you a towel. (*He starts to rise.*)

MAYA (*looking out the window*): She'd better wait a little—I used all the hot water. (*With a laugh, to* SIGMUND:) I came tonight to take a bath!

MARCUS *laughs.*

ADRIAN: Marcus, when they arrested you . . .

MAYA (*suddenly*): Will you stop writing, for Christ's sake! Isn't there something else to talk about?

MARCUS: Why not—if he's interested?

MAYA: Are we some sick fish in a tank! (*To* ADRIAN:) Stop it! (*She gets up, goes to the drink table.*) What the hell do you expect people to *do*? What *is* it?

MARCUS: You've had enough, dear . . .

MAYA (*pouring*): I have not had enough, dear. (*She suddenly slams the glass down on the table.*) Fuck all this diplomacy! (*At* ADRIAN:) You're in no position to judge anybody! We have nothing to be ashamed of!

MARCUS (*turning away in disgust*): Oh, for God's sake . . .

MAYA: You know what he brought when he came to me? A bottle of milk!

Perplexed, MARCUS *turns to her.*

I wake up and he's in the kitchen, drinking *milk!* (*She stands before* MARCUS, *awaiting his reaction.*) A grown man!

MARCUS (*to calm her*): Well, they drink a lot of it in the States.

MAYA (*quietly, seeking to explain*): He smelled like a baby, all night.

MARCUS (*stands*): I'll make you some coffee . . .

He starts past her, but she stops him with her hand on his arm, frightened and remorseful. She kisses him.

MAYA: I'm going home. (*She takes his hand, tries to lead him toward* SIGMUND *with imperative force.*) Come, be his friend . . . you are friends, darling . . . (*The telephone in the bedroom rings. She turns up to the entrance in surprise.*) Goddamn that Hilton!

She starts toward the bedroom, but as the telephone rings again, MARCUS *goes up and exits into the bedroom. She comes to* SIGMUND.

Darling . . . (*She points up to the ceiling, speaking softly in desperation.*) I really don't think there is anything there. I would never do that to you, you know that. I think it was only to make himself interesting—he can't write anymore; it left him . . . (*In anguish:*) It left him!

SIGMUND: I know.

MAYA: He loves you, he loves you, darling! . . . (*She grips her head.*) My God, I'm sick . . .

She starts upstage as MARCUS *enters. He has a stunned look.*

She halts, seeing him, looks at him questioningly. SIGMUND *turns to look at him, and* ADRIAN. *After a moment . . .*

MARCUS (*turns to* SIGMUND *with a gesture inviting him to go to the phone*): It's Alexandra.

SIGMUND *does not move.*

. . . She wishes to speak to you.

SIGMUND *stands, confounded by Marcus's look, and goes out into the bedroom.* MARCUS *remains there, staring.*

MAYA: What?

MARCUS *is silent, staring.*

ADRIAN: Something happen?

MARCUS *crosses the stage and descends into his chair, his face transfixed by some enigma.*

MAYA (*in fright, starting up toward the bedroom*): Sigmund! . . .

SIGMUND *enters, halts, shakes his head, uttering an almost soundless laugh, his eyes alive to something incredible.*

MARCUS: They're returning his manuscript.

MAYA *claps her hands together, then crosses herself, her face between explosive joy and some terror, rigid, sobered.*

ADRIAN (*grabs* SIGMUND *by the shoulders*): Is it true?

MARCUS: She may be able to bring it when she comes.

ADRIAN: Sigmund! (*He kisses him. They look at each other and laugh.*)

SIGMUND (*half smiling*): You believe it?

ADRIAN (*taken aback*): Don't you?

SIGMUND (*laughs*): I don't know! (*He walks, dumbfounded.*) . . .

Yes, I suppose I believe. (*He suddenly laughs.*) Why not! They have made me ridiculous, therefore I must believe it.

MARCUS: Well, the main thing is, you . . .

SIGMUND: Yes, that is the main thing. I must call Elizabeth . . . (*He starts to the bedroom but looks at his watch.*) No . . . she will not yet be home.

ADRIAN (*to all*): What could it mean? (*He laughs, seeing* SIG-MUND.) You look punchy. (*He grabs him.*) Wake up! You got it back! . . . Listen, come to Paris with me . . . with the boy and Elizabeth. We'll get you a visa—you can be in New York in ten days. We'll go to my publisher, I'll break his arm, we'll get you a tremendous advance, and you're on your way.

SIGMUND (*laughing*): Wait, wait . . .

ADRIAN: Say yes! Come on! You can waste the rest of your life in this goddamned country. Jesus, why can't they steal it again tomorrow? (*To the ceiling:*) I didn't mean that about the country. But it's infuriating—they play you like a yo-yo.

SIGMUND (*sits; an aura of irony on his voice*): So, Maya . . . you are immortal again.

ADRIAN: Is *she* that character?

MAYA: Of course.

ADRIAN: She sounded terrific.

MAYA: She is the best woman he has ever written—fantastic, complicated personality. (*To* SIGMUND:) What is there to keep you now? It is enough, no?

IRINA: Is good?

MARCUS (*patting her*): Yes, very good.

SIGMUND: She is so lucky—she understands nothing. We also understand nothing—but for us is not lucky.

MAYA: We should go to Francesco's later—we should have a party.

SIGMUND (*turns to her with a faint smile*): It is strange, eh? We have such good news and we are sad.

MARCUS: It isn't sadness.

SIGMUND: Perhaps only some sort of humiliation. (*He shakes his head.*) We must admire them—they are very intelligent—they can even create unhappiness with good news.

ADRIAN (*to* MARCUS): What do you suppose happened?

MARCUS: I've no idea.

ADRIAN: It seems like a gesture of some kind. Is it?

MARCUS: I haven't the foggiest.

ADRIAN: Could it be that I was here?

MARCUS: Who knows? Of course they would like to make peace with him, it's a gesture in that sense.

SIGMUND *looks across at him.*

I think you ought to consider it that way.

SIGMUND: It is their contempt; they are laughing.

MARCUS: Not necessarily—some of them have great respect for you.

SIGMUND: No, no, they are laughing.

MAYA: Why are you such children?

SIGMUND *turns to her.*

It is not respect and it is not contempt—it is nothing.

ADRIAN: But it must mean something.

MAYA: Why? They have the power to take it and the power to give it back.

ADRIAN: Well, that's a meaning.

MAYA: You didn't know that before? When it rains you get wet—that is not exactly meaningful. (*To the three:*) There's nothing to say; it is a terrible embarrassment for geniuses, but there is simply no possible comment to be made.

SIGMUND: How is in Shakespeare? "We are like flies to little boys, they kill us for their sport."

MAYA: They are not killing you at all. Not at all.

SIGMUND: Why are you angry with me? I am not obliged to ask why something happens?

MAYA: Because you can live happily and you don't want to.

ADRIAN: It's not so simple.

MAYA: But for you it is! You are so rich, Adrian, you live so well—why must he be heroic?

ADRIAN: I've never told him to . . .

MAYA: Then tell him to get out! Be simple, be clear to him . . .

ADRIAN: I've been very clear to him . . .

MAYA: Good! (*To* SIGMUND:) So the three of us are of the same opinion, you see? Let's have a party at Francesco's . . . call Elizabeth . . . a farewell party. All right?

He looks up at her.

It is all finished, darling!

He smiles, shaking his head. She is frightened and angry.

What? What is it? What more can be said?

SIGMUND (*with a certain laughter*): Is like some sort of theatre, no? Very bad theatre—our emotions have no connection with the event. Myself also—I *must* speak, darling—I do not understand myself. I must confess, I have feeling of gratitude; *before* they have stolen my book I was never grateful. *Now* I am grateful— (*His laughter vanishes.*) I cannot accept such confusion, Maya, is very bad for my mentality. I must speak! I think we must all speak now! (*He ends looking at* MARCUS; *his anger is open.*)

MARCUS: What can I tell you? I know nothing.

SIGMUND: I am sure not, but we can speculate, perhaps? (*To* MAYA:) Please, darling—sit; we must wait for Alexandra, we have nothing to do. Please, Adrian—sit down. . . . I have some idea . . .

> ADRIAN *sits.* SIGMUND *continues to* MAYA.

. . . which I would like to discuss before I leave my country.

> MAYA *sits slowly, apprehensively. He turns to* MARCUS, *adopting a quiet, calm air.*

Is possible, Marcus—there was some sort of mistake? Perhaps only one police commander has made this decision for himself—to stealing my book? Perhaps the government was also surprised?

> MARCUS *considers in silence.*

I am interested your opinion. *I* think so, perhaps—no?

MARCUS: Do you know if they were the Security Police?

SIGMUND: Yes, Security Police.

MARCUS: *They* might, I suppose.

SIGMUND: I think so. But in this case . . . this fellow in London taxi—is possible he was also speaking for himself?

MARCUS: I can't believe that.

SIGMUND: But if he was speaking for government . . . such terrible thing against me—why have they chosen to returning my manuscript? I think is not logical, no?

MARCUS: . . . Unless they had second thoughts, and felt it would make it easier for you to leave.

SIGMUND: Yes. That is very strong idea.

ADRIAN: I think that's it.

SIGMUND: Very good, yes. But at same time, if I have manuscript—you do not object that I . . . ?

MARCUS: Go ahead—it's simply that I know no more than . . .

SIGMUND: You understand is very important to me. . . . I must understand why I am leaving.

MARCUS: Of course. Go ahead.

SIGMUND (*slight pause*): If I have manuscript, I must probably conclude is *not* dangerous for me here, no? I must believe is only some particular antagonistic enemy who wish me to go out. Is possible?

MARCUS: What can I tell you?

SIGMUND (*with nearly an outcry through his furious control*): But you know you are sad! I am sad, Maya is sad—if was some sort of mistake . . . why we are not happy?

MAYA *gets up and strides toward the bedroom.*

Maya?

MAYA (*hardly turning back*): I'm going home . . .

SIGMUND (*leaps up and intercepts her*): No, no—we must have celebration! (*He grips her hands.*)

MAYA: Let me go!

SIGMUND: No! We have tremendous good news, we must have correct emotion!

MAYA (*wrenching her hands free, pointing at his pocket*): Give me that thing. . . . Give it to me!

SIGMUND: My God—I had forgotten it. (*He takes out the pistol, looks at it.*)

MAYA: Please. Sigmund. Please! . . .

SIGMUND: I have crazy idea . . .

MAYA (*weeping*): Sigmund . . .

SIGMUND (*moving toward the piano*): One time very long ago, I have read in American detective story . . . that criminal has placed revolver inside piano. (*He sets the pistol on the strings and comes around to the bench.*) Then someone is playing very fortissimo . . . something like Beethoven . . . (*raising his hands over the keyboard*) . . . and he is firing the pistol.

ADRIAN: What the hell are you doing?

SIGMUND (*smashes his hands down on the keyboard*): Ha! Is not true.

ADRIAN (*stands*): What the hell are you doing?

SIGMUND: Wait! I have idea . . . (*He reaches over, takes out the pistol, and cocks it.*)

MAYA: Marcus!

SIGMUND (*replacing the cocked pistol in the piano*): Now we shall see . . .

ADRIAN (*rushing MAYA away from the piano*): Watch out!

SIGMUND (*crashes his hands down; the gun explodes, the strings *reverberate*): Is true! (*He reaches in and takes up the revolver.*) My God, I am so happy . . . (*He holds up the revolver.*) The truth is alive in our country, Marcus! (*He comes and sits near* MARCUS.) Is unmistakable, no?—when something is true?

He looks at the pistol, puts it in his pocket. MARCUS *turns to him only now.* MAYA *suddenly weeps, sobbing, and makes for the bedroom.*

I cannot permit you to leave, Maya!

She halts, turning to him in terror.

I must insist, darling—is most important evening of my life, and I understand nothing. Why do you weep, why do you go? If I am ridiculous I must understand why! Please . . . sit. Perhaps you can say something.

She sits a distance from him and MARCUS. ADRIAN *remains standing, catching his breath; he leans his head on his hand, as though caught by a rush of sadness, and he shakes his head incredulously, glancing at* MARCUS.

MARCUS: What is it? What *is* it!

SIGMUND: This fellow . . . this fellow in taxi who has threatened me—what was his name?

MARCUS: I don't recall, I only heard it once. Granitz, I think. Or Grodnitz. But I'm sure he didn't know you.

SIGMUND: Grodnitz.

MARCUS: . . . Or Granitz.

ADRIAN: You know him?

SIGMUND: . . . No. (*Slight pause.*) No Granitz. No Grodnitz. (*Slight pause. He takes the pistol out of his pocket, looks at it in his hand, then turns again to* MARCUS.) He exists? Or is imaginary man?

MARCUS *is silent.*

Was *ever* discussion of trial for me? Or is imaginary trial?

MARCUS *is silent.* SIGMUND *looks at the pistol again; then, stretching over to* MARCUS, *he places it in his hand.*

I believe I have no danger, at the moment.

Long pause. No one dares do more than glance at MARCUS, *whose face is filled with his fury. The pause lengthens.* SIGMUND *looks at his watch.*

I will try to call Elizabeth.

MARCUS: The sole function of every other writer is to wish he were you.

SIGMUND *stands and looks to* MAYA, *who avoids his eyes. He exits into the bedroom. After a moment . . .*

ADRIAN (*sotto, to assuage* MARCUS): He's terribly scared . . .

MARCUS (*slight pause; like a final verdict*): I couldn't care less. (*He looks at his watch.*)

ADRIAN (*silent for a moment*): For what it's worth . . . I know he has tremendous feeling for you.

MARCUS: For his monument. To build his monument he has to prove that everyone else is a coward or corrupt. My mistake was to offer him my help—it's a menace to his lonely grandeur. No one is permitted anything but selfishness. He's insane.

ADRIAN: Oh, come on . . .

MARCUS: He's paranoid—these letters to the foreign press are for nothing but to bring on another confrontation. It was too peaceful; they were threatening him with tolerance. He must find evil or he can't be good.

MAYA: Let's not talk about it anymore . . .

MARCUS: I exist too, Maya! I am not dancing around that mega-lomania again.

Slight pause.

ADRIAN: I can't blame you, but I wish you wouldn't cut out on him yet. Look, I'll stay through the week, maybe I can convince him. Does he have a week?

MARCUS (*slowly turns to* ADRIAN): How would I know?

ADRIAN: All I meant was whether you . . .

MARCUS: I won't have any more of this, Adrian!

Slight pause.

ADRIAN: I believe you—I've told him to get out.

MARCUS: No, you haven't; you've insinuated.

ADRIAN: Christ's sake, you've heard me say . . .

MARCUS: I *have* heard you.

They are facing each other. Slight pause.

You don't believe me, Adrian . . . not really.

ADRIAN *can't answer.*

So it's all over. It's the end of him—I've been there. He will smash his head against the walls, and the rest of us will pay for his grandeur.

Slight pause. ADRIAN *turns front in his conflict.* SIGMUND *enters.* MARCUS *turns away.*

MAYA (*with a forced attempt at cheerfulness*): Did you reach her? Elizabeth?

SIGMUND: She is very happy. (*To* MARCUS:) She send you her greetings—she is grateful. (*Slight pause.*) I also.

MARCUS *half turns toward him.* SIGMUND *says no more, goes to his chair and sits.*

ADRIAN: Sigmund? (SIGMUND *glances at him.*) Do you trust me?

SIGMUND *is silent.*

I'm convinced he's told you the truth.

SIGMUND *is silent.*

In all the times we've talked about you, he's never shown anything but a wide-open pride in you, and your work. He's with you. You have to believe that.

SIGMUND *turns, stares at Marcus's profile for a moment, then looks at* MAYA. *She ultimately turns slightly away. He looks down at the floor.*

SIGMUND: I am afraid; that is all. I think I will not be able to write in some other country.

ADRIAN: Oh, that's impossible . . .

SIGMUND: I am not cosmopolitan writer, I am provincial writer. I believe I must hear my language every day, I must walk in these particular streets. I think in New York I will have only some terrible silence. Is like old tree—it is difficult to moving old tree, they most probably die.

ADRIAN: But if they lock you up . . .

SIGMUND: Yes, but that is my fate; I must accept my fate. But to run away because of some sort of rumor—I have only some rumor, no? How will I support this silence that I have brought on myself? This is terrible idea, no? How I can accept to be so ridiculous? Therefore, is reasonable, I believe—that I must absolutely understand who is speaking to me.

ADRIAN (*slight pause, a hesitation*): I'm going to level with you, Sigmund—I think you're being far too . . .

SIGMUND (*a frustrated outburst*): I am not crazy, Adrian! (*All turn to him, fear in their faces. He spreads his arms, with an upward glance.*) Who is commanding me? Who is this voice? *Who is speaking to me?*

MAYA: They. (*An instant's silence; she seems ashamed to look directly at* SIGMUND. *She gestures almost imperceptibly upward.*) It is there.

MARCUS (*in protest*): Maya!

MAYA: Why not! (*To* SIGMUND:) They have heard it all.

MARCUS (*to* SIGMUND *and* ADRIAN): It isn't true, there's nothing.

MAYA (*persisting, to* SIGMUND): He has risked everything . . . for you. God knows what will happen for what has been said here.

MARCUS (*to* SIGMUND): There's nothing . . . she can't know . . . (*To* MAYA:) You can't know that . . .

MAYA (*her eyes to the ceiling*): Who else have we been speaking to all evening! (*To them all:*) Who does not believe it? (*To* MARCUS:) It is his life, darling—we must begin to say what we believe. Somewhere, we must begin!

> *Pause. She sits a distance from* SIGMUND; *only after a moment does she turn to face him as she fights down her shame and her fear of him.*

SIGMUND: So.

MAYA (*downing her shame*): Just so, yes. You must go.

SIGMUND: For your sake.

MAYA: Yes.

MARCUS (*softly, facing front*): It isn't true.

MAYA: And yours. For all of us.

SIGMUND: You must . . . deliver me? My departure?

MAYA *stiffens. She cannot speak.*

For your program? His passport? . . .

ADRIAN: Sigmund, it's enough . . .

MAYA: He had no need to return, except he loves you. There was no need. That is also true.

SIGMUND (*his head clamped in his hands*): My God . . . Maya. (*Pause. To* MARCUS:) They brought you back to make sure my departure?

ADRIAN (*aborting the violence coming*): Come on, Sigmund, it's enough . . .

SIGMUND (*trying to laugh*): But she is not some sort of whore! I have many years with this woman! . . .

ADRIAN: What more do you *want!*

MARCUS: Her humiliation; she's not yet on her knees to him. We are now to take our places, you see, at the foot of the cross, as he floats upward through the plaster on the wings of his immortal contempt. We lack remorse, it spoils the picture. (*He glares, smiling at* SIGMUND, *who seems on the verge of springing at him.*)

ADRIAN (*to* SIGMUND): Forget it, Sigmund—come on . . . (*To* MARCUS:) Maybe you ought to call that Alexandra woman.

MARCUS: She'll be along.

> *Silence. The moment expands.* SIGMUND *stares front, gripping his lower face.* ADRIAN *is glancing at him with apprehension.* MAYA *is looking at no one.*

SIGMUND (*to* MAYA): You can say nothing to me?

MAYA (*slight pause*): You know my feeling.

SIGMUND: I, not. I know your name. Who is this woman?

MARCUS: Don't play that game with him.

SIGMUND: It is a game?

ADRIAN: Come on, fellas . . .

SIGMUND (*irritated, to* ADRIAN): Is interesting to me. (*To* MARCUS:) What is your game? What did you mean?

MARCUS: It's called Power. Or Moral Monopoly. The winner takes all the justifications. When you write this, Adrian, I hope you include the fact that they refused him a visa for many years and he was terribly indignant—the right to leave was sacred to civilization. Now he has that right and it's an insult. You can draw your own conclusions.

SIGMUND: And what is the conclusion?

MARCUS: You are a moral blackmailer. We have all humored you, Sigmund, out of some misplaced sense of responsibility to our literature. Or maybe it's only our terror of vanishing altogether. We aren't the Russians—after you and Otto and Peter there aren't a handful to keep the breath of life in this language. We have taken all the responsibility and left you all the freedom to call us morally bankrupt. But now you're free to go, so the responsibility moves to you. Now it's yours. All yours. We have done what was possible; now you will do what is necessary, or turn out our lights. And that is where it stands.

SIGMUND (*slight pause*): This is all?

   MARCUS *is silent.*

ADRIAN: What more can be said, Sigmund? What can they give you? It's pointless.

SIGMUND (*turns to* MAYA): What you can give me, Maya? (*She is silent.*) There is nothing? I am only some sort of . . . comical Jesus Christ? Is only my egotism? This is all?

In silence, MAYA *turns to face him.*

You understand what I ask you?

MAYA: Yes.

SIGMUND: You cannot? (*Slight pause. Then he glances toward* MARCUS.) After so many years . . . so many conversations . . . so many hope and disaster—you can only speak for them? (*He gestures toward the ceiling.*) Is terrible, no? Why we have lived?

ADRIAN (*to cut off his mounting anger*): Sigmund . . .

SIGMUND (*swiftly, his eyes blazing*): Why have you come here? What do you want in this country?

ADRIAN (*astonished*): What the hell are you . . .

SIGMUND: You are scientist observing the specimens: this whore? this clever fellow making business with these gangsters?

ADRIAN: For Christ's sake, Sigmund, what can I do!

SIGMUND: They are killing us, Adrian—they have destroyed my friends! You are free man— (*with a gesture toward the ceiling*) why you are obliged to be clever? Why do you come here, Adrian?

MAYA: To save his book.

ADRIAN: That's a lie!

MAYA: But it's exactly what you told me an hour ago. (*She stands. To both* SIGMUND *and* ADRIAN:) What is the sin? He has come for his profit, to rescue two years' work, to make more money . . .

ADRIAN: That's a goddamned lie!

MAYA: And for friendship! Oh, yes—his love for you. I believe it! Like ours. Absolutely like ours! Is love not love because there is some profit in it? Who speaks only for his heart? And yes, I speak to them now—this moment, this very moment to them, that they may have mercy on my program, on his passport. Always to them, in some part to them for my profit—here and everywhere in this world! Just as you do.

SIGMUND: I speak for Sigmund.

MAYA: Only Sigmund? Then why can't you speak for Sigmund in America? Because you will not have them in America to hate! And if you cannot hate you cannot write and you will not be Sigmund anymore, but another lousy refugee ordering his chicken soup in broken English—and where is the profit in that? They are your theme, your life, your partner in this dance that cannot stop or you will die of silence! (*She moves toward him. Tenderly:*) They are in you, darling. And if you stay . . . it is also for your profit . . . as it is for ours to tell you to go. Who can speak for himself alone?

> *A heavy brass knocker is heard from below.* SIGMUND *lifts his eyes to the ceiling.* MARCUS *stands and faces* SIGMUND, *who now turns to him. Silence.*

SIGMUND: Tell her, please . . . is impossible . . . any transaction. Only to return my property.

MAYA (*with an abjectness, a terror, taking his hand and kissing it*): Darling . . . for my sake. For this little life that I have made . . .

MARCUS (*with anger, disgust*): Stop it! (*He turns to* SIGMUND.) For your monument. For the bowing ushers in the theatre. For the power . . . the power to bring down everyone.

SIGMUND (*spreads his hands, looks up at the ceiling*): I don't know. (*He turns to* MARCUS.) But I will never leave. Never.

> *Another knock is heard.* MARCUS, *his face set, goes out and up the corridor.* SIGMUND *turns to* MAYA. *She walks away, her face expressionless, and stands at the window staring out.*

Forgive me, Maya.

She doesn't turn to him. He looks to ADRIAN.

Is quite simple. We are ridiculous people now. And when we try to escape it, we are ridiculous too.

ADRIAN: No.

SIGMUND: I think so. But we cannot help ourselves. I must give you . . . certain letters, I wish you to keep them . . . before you leave. (*He sits.*) I have one some years ago from Malraux. Very elegant. *French,* you know? Also Gyula Illyes, Hungarian . . . very wise fellow. Heinrich Böll, Germany, one letter. Kobo Abe, Japan— he also. Nadine Gordimer, South Africa. Also Cortázar, Argentina . . . (*Slight pause.*) My God, eh? So many writers! Like snow . . . like forest . . . these enormous trees everywhere on the earth. Marvelous. (*Slight pause. A welling up in him. He suddenly cries out to* MAYA *across the stage.*) Maya! Forgive me . . . (*He hurries to her.*) I cannot help it.

MAYA: I know. (*She turns to him, reaches out and touches his face.*) Thank you.

SIGMUND (*surprised, he is motionless for an instant, then pulls her into his arms and holds her face*): Oh, my God! Thank you, Maya.

The voices of MARCUS *and* ALEXANDRA *are heard approaching from the darkness up the corridor. The three of them turn toward the door.*

IRINA (*revolving her finger, to* MAYA): Now, music?

CURTAIN

The American Clock

A VAUDEVILLE

Based in part on Studs Terkel's *Hard Times*.

CHARACTERS

THEODORE K. QUINN

LEE BAUM

ROSE BAUM, Lee's mother

MOE BAUM, Lee's father

ARTHUR A. ROBERTSON

CLARENCE, a shoeshine man

FRANK, the Baums' chauffeur

FANNY MARGOLIES, Rose's sister

GRANDPA, Rose's father

DR. ROSMAN

Financiers { JESSE LIVERMORE / WILLIAM DURANT / ARTHUR CLAYTON

TONY, a speakeasy owner

DIANA MORGAN

HENRY TAYLOR, a farmer

IRENE, a middle-aged black woman

BANKS, a black veteran

JOE, a boyhood friend of Lee's

MRS. TAYLOR, Henry's wife

HARRIET TAYLOR, their daughter

Farmers { BREWSTER / CHARLEY

JUDGE BRADLEY

FRANK HOWARD, an auctioneer

MISS FOWLER, Quinn's secretary
GRAHAM, a *New York Times* reporter
SIDNEY MARGOLIES, Fanny's son
DORIS GROSS, the landlady's daughter

Students $\begin{cases} \text{RALPH} \\ \text{RUDY} \end{cases}$

ISABEL, a prostitute
ISAAC, a black café proprietor
RYAN, a federal relief supervisor

People at the relief office $\begin{cases} \text{MATTHEW R. BUSH} \\ \text{GRACE} \\ \text{KAPUSH} \\ \text{DUGAN} \\ \text{TOLAND} \\ \text{LUCY} \end{cases}$

EDIE, a comic-strip artist
LUCILLE, Rose's niece
STANISLAUS, a seaman
BASEBALL PLAYER
WAITER
THIEF
FARMERS
BIDDERS
SHERIFF
DEPUTIES
MARATHON DANCERS
WELFARE WORKER
SOLDIERS

ACT ONE

The set is a flexible area for actors. The actors are seated in a choral area onstage and return to it when their scenes are over. The few pieces of furniture required should be openly carried on by the actors. An impression of a surrounding vastness should be given, as though the whole country were really the setting, even as the intimacy of certain scenes is provided for. The background can be sky, clouds, space itself, or an impression of the geography of the United States.

A small jazz band onstage plays "Million-Dollar Baby" as a baseball pitcher enters, tossing a ball from hand to glove. QUINN *begins to whistle "Million-Dollar Baby" from the balcony. Now he sings, and the rest of the company joins in, gradually coming onstage. All are singing by the end of the verse. All form in positions onstage. The band remains onstage throughout the play.*

ROSE: By the summer of 1929 . . .

LEE: I think it's fair to say that nearly every American . . .

MOE: Firmly believed that he was going to get . . .

COMPANY: Richer and richer . . .

MOE: Every year.

ROBERTSON: The country knelt to a golden calf in a blanket of red, white, and blue. (*He walks to Clarence's shoeshine box.*) How you making out, Clarence?

CLARENCE: Mr. Robertson, I like you to lay another ten dollars on that General Electric. You do that for me?

106

ROBERTSON: How much stock you own, Clarence?

CLARENCE: Well, this ten ought to buy me a thousand dollars' worth, so altogether I guess I got me about hundred thousand dollars in stock.

ROBERTSON: And how much cash you got home?

CLARENCE: Oh, I guess about forty, forty-five dollars.

ROBERTSON (*slight pause*): All right, Clarence, let me tell you something. But I want you to promise me not to repeat it to anyone.

CLARENCE: I never repeat a tip you give me, Mr. Robertson.

ROBERTSON: This isn't quite a tip, this is what you might call an un-tip. Take all your stock, and sell it.

CLARENCE: Sell! Why, just this morning in the paper Mr. Andrew Mellon say the market's got to keep goin' up. *Got* to!

ROBERTSON: I have great respect for Andrew Mellon, Clarence, know him well, but he's up to his eyebrows in this game—he's got to say that. You sell, Clarence, believe me.

CLARENCE (*drawing himself up*): I never like to criticize a customer, Mr. Robertson, but I don't think a man in your position ought to be carryin' on that kind of talk! Now you take this ten, sir, put it on General Electric for Clarence.

ROBERTSON: I tell you something funny, Clarence.

CLARENCE: What's that, sir?

ROBERTSON: You sound like every banker in the United States.

CLARENCE: Well, I should hope so!

ROBERTSON: Yeah, well . . . bye-bye.

He exits. CLARENCE *exits with his shoeshine box. The company exits singing and humming "Million-Dollar Baby";* QUINN *sings the final line.*

Light rises on ROSE *at the piano, dressed for an evening out. Two valises stand center stage.*

ROSE (*playing piano under speech*): Now sing, darling, but don't forget to breathe—and then you'll do your homework.

LEE (*starts singing "I Can't Give You Anything But Love," then speaks over music*): Up to '29 it was the age of belief. How could Lindbergh fly the Atlantic in that tiny little plane? He believed. How could Babe Ruth keep smashing those homers? He believed. Charley Paddock, "The World's Fastest Human," raced a racehorse . . . and won! Because he believed. What I believed at fourteen was that my mother's hair was supposed to flow down over her shoulders. And one afternoon she came into the apartment . . .

> ROSE, *at piano, sings a line of "I Can't Give You Anything But Love."*

. . . and it was short!

> ROSE *and* LEE *sing the last line together.*

ROSE (*continuing to play, speaking over music*): I personally think with all the problems there was never such a glorious time for anybody who loved to play or sing or listen or dance to music. It seems to me every week there was another marvelous song. What's the matter with you?

> LEE *can only shake his head—"nothing."*

Oh, for God's sake! Nobody going to bother with long hair anymore. All I was doing was winding it up and winding it down . . .

LEE: It's *okay*! I just didn't think it would ever . . . happen.

ROSE: But why can't there be something new!

LEE: But why didn't you *tell* me!

ROSE: Because you would do exactly what you're doing now—carrying on like I was some kind of I-don't-know-what! Now stop being an idiot and *sing*!

> LEE *starts singing "On the Sunny Side of the Street."*

You're not breathing, dear.

> MOE *enters carrying a telephone, joins in song.* LEE *continues singing under dialogue.*

ROSE: Rudy Vallee is turning green.

> FRANK *enters in a chauffeur's uniform.*

MOE (*into phone*): Trafalgar five, seven-seven-one-one. (*Pause.*) Herb? I'm just thinking, maybe I ought to pick up another five hundred shares of General Electric. (*Pause.*) Good. (*He hangs up.*)

FRANK: Car's ready, Mr. Baum.

> FRANK *chimes in with* LEE *on the last line of "Sunny Side of the Street." Then* LEE *sits on the floor, working on his crystal set.*

ROSE (*to* FRANK): You'll drop us at the theatre and then take my father and sister to Brooklyn and come back for us after the show. And don't get lost, please.

FRANK: No, I know Brooklyn.

> *He exits with the baggage.* FANNY *enters—*ROSE'*s sister.*

FANNY (*apprehensively*): Rose . . . listen . . . Papa really doesn't want to move in with us.

A slow turn with rising eyebrows from MOE; ROSE *is likewise alarmed.*

ROSE (*to* FANNY): Don't be silly, he's been with us six months.

FANNY (*fearfully, voice lowered*): I'm telling you . . . he is not happy about it.

MOE (*resoundingly understating the irony*): He's not happy.

FANNY (*to* MOE): Well, you know how he loves space, and this apartment is so roomy.

MOE (*to* LEE): He bought himself a grave, you know. It's going to be in the cemetery on the aisle. So he'll have a little more room to move around, . . .

ROSE: Oh, stop it.

MOE: . . . get in and out quicker.

FANNY (*innocently*): Out of a grave?

ROSE: He's kidding you, for God's sake!

FANNY: Oh! (*To* ROSE:) I think he's afraid my house'll be too small; you know, with Sidney and us and the one bathroom. And what is he going to do with himself in Brooklyn? He never liked the country.

ROSE: Fanny, dear, make up your mind—he's going to *love* it with you.

MOE: Tell you, Fanny—maybe we should *all* move over to your house and he could live here with an eleven-room apartment for himself, and we'll send the maid every day to do his laundry . . .

FANNY: He's brushing his hair, Rose, but I know he's not happy. I think what it is, he still misses Mama, you see.

MOE: Now *that's* serious—a man his age still misses his mother . . .

FANNY: No, *our* mother—*Mama*. (*To* ROSE, *almost laughing, pointing at* MOE:) He thought Papa misses his own mother!

ROSE: No, he didn't, he's kidding you!

FANNY: Oh, you . . . ! (*She swipes at* MOE.)

ROSE (*walking her to the doorway*): Go hurry him up. I don't want to miss the first scene of this show; it's Gershwin, it's supposed to be wonderful.

FANNY: See, what it is, something is always happening here . . .

MOE (*into phone*): Trafalgar five, seven-seven-one-one.

FANNY: . . . I mean with the stock market and the business. . . . Papa just loves all this!

> GRANDPA *appears, in a suit, with a cane; very neat, proper— and very sorry for himself. Comes to a halt, already hurt.*

MOE (*to* GRANDPA): See you again soon, Charley!

FANNY (*deferentially*): You ready, Papa?

MOE (*on phone*): Herb? . . . Maybe I ought to get rid of my Worthington Pump. Oh . . . thousand shares? And remind me to talk to you about gold, will you? (*Pause.*) Good. (*He hangs up.*)

FANNY (*with* ROSE, *getting* GRANDPA *into his coat*): Rose'll come every few days, Papa . . .

ROSE: Sunday we'll all come out and spend the day.

GRANDPA: Brooklyn is full of tomatoes.

FANNY: No, they're starting to put up big apartment houses now; it's practically not the country anymore. (*In a tone of happy reassurance:*) On some streets there's hardly a tree! (*To* ROSE, *of her diamond bracelet:*) I'm looking at that bracelet! Is it new?

ROSE: For my birthday.

FANNY: It's gorgeous.

ROSE: He gave exactly the same one to his mother.

FANNY: She must be overjoyed.

ROSE (*with a cutting smile, to* MOE): Why not?

GRANDPA (*making a sudden despairing announcement*): Well? So I'm going! (*With a sharp tap of his cane on the floor, he starts off.*)

LEE: Bye-bye, Grandpa!

GRANDPA (*goes to* LEE, *offers his cheek, gets his kiss, then pinches Lee's cheek*): You be a good boy. (*He strides past* ROSE, *huffily snatches his hat out of her hand, and exits.*)

MOE: There goes the boarder. I lived to see it!

ROSE (*to* LEE): Want to come and ride with us?

LEE: I think I'll stay and work on my radio.

ROSE: Good, and go to bed early. I'll bring home all the music from the show, and we'll sing it tomorrow. (*She kisses* LEE.) Good night, darling. (*She swings out in her furs.*)

MOE (*to* LEE): Whyn't you get a haircut?

LEE: I did, but it grew back, I think.

MOE (*realizing Lee's size*): Should you talk to your mother about college or something?

LEE: Oh, no, not for a couple of years.

MOE: Oh. Okay, good. (*He laughs and goes out, perfectly at one with the world.*)

> ROBERTSON *appears, walks over to the couch, and lies down.* DR. ROSMAN *appears and sits in a chair behind Robertson's head.*

ROBERTSON: Where'd I leave off yesterday?

DR. ROSMAN: Your mother had scalded the cat.

>   *Pause.*

ROBERTSON: There's something else, Doctor. I feel a conflict about saying it . . .

DR. ROSMAN: That's what we're here for.

ROBERTSON: I don't mean in the usual sense. It has to do with money.

DR. ROSMAN: Yes?

ROBERTSON: Your money.

DR. ROSMAN (*turns down to him, alarmed*): What about it?

ROBERTSON (*hesitates*): I think you ought to get out of the market.

DR. ROSMAN: Out of the market!

ROBERTSON: Sell everything.

DR. ROSMAN (*pauses, raises his head to think, then speaks carefully*): Could you talk about the basis for this idea? When was the first time you had this thought?

ROBERTSON: About four months ago. Around the middle of May.

DR. ROSMAN: Can you recall what suggested it?

ROBERTSON: One of my companies manufactures kitchen utensils.

DR. ROSMAN: The one in Indiana?

ROBERTSON: Yes. In the middle of May all our orders stopped.

DR. ROSMAN: Completely?

ROBERTSON: Dead stop. It's now the end of August, and they haven't resumed.

DR. ROSMAN: How is that possible? The stock keeps going up.

ROBERTSON: Thirty points in less than two months. This is what I've been trying to tell you for a long time now, Doctor—the market represents nothing but a state of mind. (*He sits up.*) On the other hand, I must face the possibility that this is merely my personal fantasy . . .

DR. ROSMAN: Yes, your fear of approaching disaster.

ROBERTSON: But I've had meetings at the Morgan Bank all week, and it's the same in almost every industry—it's not just my companies. The warehouses are overflowing, we can't move the goods, that's an objective fact.

DR. ROSMAN: Have you told your thoughts to your colleagues?

ROBERTSON: They won't listen. Maybe they can't afford to—we've been tossing the whole country onto a crap table in a game where nobody is ever supposed to lose! . . . I sold off a lot two years ago, but when the market opens tomorrow I'm cashing in the rest. I feel guilty for it, but I can't see any other way.

DR. ROSMAN: Why does selling make you feel guilty?

ROBERTSON: Dumping twelve million dollars in securities could start a slide. It could wipe out thousands of widows and old people. . . . I've even played with the idea of making a public announcement.

DR. ROSMAN: That you're dumping twelve million dollars? That could start a slide all by itself, couldn't it?

ROBERTSON: But it would warn the little people.

DR. ROSMAN: Yes, but selling out quietly might not disturb the market quite so much. You *could* be wrong, too.

ROBERTSON: I suppose so. Yes. . . . Maybe I'll just sell and shut up. You're right. I could be mistaken.

DR. ROSMAN (*relieved*): You probably are—but I think I'll sell out anyway.

ROBERTSON: Fine, Doctor. (*He stands, straightens his jacket.*) And one more thing. This is going to sound absolutely nuts, but . . . when you get your cash, don't keep it. Buy gold.

DR. ROSMAN: You can't be serious.

ROBERTSON: Gold bars, Doctor. The dollar may disappear with the rest of it. (*He extends his hand.*) Well, good luck.

DR. ROSMAN: Your hand is shaking.

ROBERTSON: Why not? Ask any two great bankers in the United States and they'd say that Arthur A. Robertson had lost his mind. (*Pause.*) Gold bars, Doctor . . . and don't put them in the bank. In the basement. Take care, now. (*He exits.*)

A bar. People in evening dress seated morosely at tables. An atmosphere of shock and even embarrassment.

LIVERMORE: About Randolph Morgan. Could you actually see him falling?

TONY: Oh, yeah. It was still that blue light, just before it gets dark? And I don't know why, something made me look up. And there's a man flyin' spread-eagle, falling through the air. He was right on top of me, like a giant! (*He looks down.*) And I look. I couldn't believe it. It's Randolph!

LIVERMORE: Poor, poor man.

DURANT: Damned fool.

LIVERMORE: I don't know—I think there is a certain gallantry . . . When you lose other people's money as well as your own, there can be no other way out.

DURANT: There's always a way out. The door.

TONY: Little more brandy, Mr. Durant?

LIVERMORE (*raising his cup*): To Randolph Morgan.

> DURANT *raises his cup.*

TONY: Amen here. And I want to say something else—everybody should get down on their knees and thank John D. Rockefeller.

LIVERMORE: Now you're talking.

TONY: Honest to God, Mr. Livermore, didn't that shoot a thrill in you? I mean, there's a *man*—to come out like that with the whole market falling to pieces and say, "I and my sons are buying six million dollars in common stocks." I mean, that's a bullfighter.

LIVERMORE: He'll turn it all around, too.

TONY: Sure he'll turn it around, because the man's a capitalist, he knows how to put up a battle. You wait, tomorrow morning it'll all be shootin' up again like Roman candles!

> *Enter* WAITER, *who whispers in Tony's ear.*

Sure, sure, bring her in.

> WAITER *hurries out.* TONY *turns to the two financiers.*

My God, it's Randolph's sister. . . . She don't know yet.

> *Enter* DIANA, *a young woman of elegant ease.*

How do you do, Miss Morgan, come in, come in. Here, I got a nice table for you.

DIANA (*all bright Southern belle*): Thank you!

TONY: Can I bring you nice steak? Little drink?

DIANA: I believe I'll wait for Mr. Robertson.

TONY: Sure. Make yourself at home.

DIANA: Are you the . . . *famous* Tony?

TONY: That's right, miss.

DIANA: I certainly am thrilled to meet you. I've read all about this marvelous place. (*She looks around avidly.*) Are all these people literary?

TONY: Well, not all, Miss Morgan.

DIANA: But this is the speakeasy F. Scott Fitzgerald frequents, isn't it?

TONY: Oh, yeah, but tonight is very quiet with the stock market and all, people stayin' home a lot the last couple days.

DIANA: Is that gentleman a writer?

TONY: No, miss, that's Jake the Barber, he's in the liquor business.

DIANA: And these?

> *She points to* DURANT *and* LIVERMORE. DURANT, *having overheard, stands.*

TONY: Mr. Durant, Miss Morgan. Mr. Livermore, Miss Morgan.

DIANA (*in a Southern accent, to the audience*): The name of Jesse Livermore was uttered in my family like the name of a genius! A Shakespeare, a Dante of corporate finance.

> CLAYTON, *at the bar, picks up a phone.*

LEE (*looking on from choral area*): And William Durant . . . he had a car named after him, the Durant Six.

MOE (*beside* LEE): A *car*? Durant had control of General Motors, for God's sake.

DIANA: Not *the* Jesse Livermore?

LIVERMORE: Afraid so, yes!

DIANA: Well, I declare! And sitting here just like two ordinary millionaires!

LEE: Ah, yes, the Great Men. The fabled High Priests of the never-ending Boom.

DIANA: This is certainly a banner evening for me! . . . I suppose you know Durham quite well.

LIVERMORE: Durham? I don't believe I've ever been there.

DIANA: But your big Philip Morris plant is there. You do still own Philip Morris, don't you?

LIVERMORE: Oh, yes, but to bet on a horse there's no need to ride him. I never mix in business. I am only interested in stocks.

DIANA: Well, that's sort of miraculous, isn't it, to own a place like that and never've seen it! My brother's in brokerage—Randolph Morgan?

LIVERMORE: I dealt with Randolph when I bought the controlling shares in IBM. Fine fellow.

DIANA: But I don't understand why he'd be spending the night in his office. The market's closed at night, isn't it?

Both men shift uneasily.

DURANT: Oh, yes, but there's an avalanche of selling orders from all over the country, and they're working round the clock to tally them up. The truth is, there's not a price on anything at the moment. In fact, Mr. Clayton over there at the end of the bar is waiting for the latest estimates.

DIANA: I'm sure something will be done, won't there? (*She laughs.*) They've cut off our telephone!

LIVERMORE: How's that?

DIANA: It seems that Daddy's lived on loans the last few months and his credit stopped. I had no idea! (*She laughs.*) I feel like a figure in a dream. I sat down in the dining car the other day, absolutely famished, and realized I had only forty cents! I am surviving on chocolate bars! (*Her charm barely hides her anxiety.*) Whatever has become of all the money?

LIVERMORE: You mustn't worry, Miss Morgan, there'll soon be plenty of money. Money is like a shy bird: the slightest rustle in the trees and it flies for cover. But money cannot bear solitude for long, it must come out and feed. And that is why we must all speak positively and show our confidence.

ROSE (*from choral area*): And they were nothing but pickpockets in a crowd of innocent pilgrims.

LIVERMORE: With Rockefeller's announcement this morning the climb has probably begun already.

ROBERTSON (*from choral area*): Yes, but they also believed.

TAYLOR (*from choral area*): *What* did they believe?

IRENE and BANKS (*from choral area, echoing* TAYLOR): Yeah, what did they believe?

ROBERTSON: Why, the most important thing of all—that talk makes facts!

DURANT: If I were you, Miss Morgan, I would prepare myself for the worst.

LIVERMORE: Now, Bill, there is no good in that kind of talk.

ROBERTSON: And they ended up believing it themselves!

DURANT: It's far more dreamlike than you imagine, Miss Morgan.

MOE: There they are, chatting away, while the gentleman at the end of the bar . . .

DURANT: . . . That gentleman . . . who has just put down the telephone is undoubtedly steeling himself to tell me that I have lost control of General Motors.

DIANA: What!

CLAYTON, *at the bar, has indeed put down the phone, has straightened his vest, and is now crossing to their table.*

DURANT (*watching him approach*): If I were you, I'd muster all the strength I have, Miss Morgan. Yes, Clayton?

CLAYTON: If we could talk privately, sir . . .

DURANT: Am I through?

CLAYTON: If you could borrow for two or three weeks . . .

DURANT: From whom?

CLAYTON: I don't know, sir.

DURANT (*standing*): Good night, Miss Morgan.

She is looking up at him, astonished.

How old are you?

DIANA: Nineteen.

DURANT: I hope you will look things in the face, young lady. Shun paper. Paper is the plague. Good luck to you. (*He turns to go.*)

LIVERMORE: We have to talk, Bill . . .

DURANT: Nothing to say, Jesse. Go to bed, old boy. It's long past midnight.

MOE (*trying to recall*): Say . . . didn't Durant end up managing a bowling alley in Toledo, Ohio?

CLAYTON (*nods*): Dead broke.

LIVERMORE (*turns to* CLAYTON, *adopting a tone of casual challenge*): Clayton . . . what's Philip Morris going to open at, can they tell?

CLAYTON: Below twenty. No higher. If we can find buyers at all.

LIVERMORE (*his smile gone*): But Rockefeller. Rockefeller . . .

CLAYTON: It doesn't seem to have had any effect, sir.

> LIVERMORE *stands. Pause.*

I should get back to the office, sir, if I may.

> LIVERMORE *is silent.*

I'm very sorry, Mr. Livermore.

> CLAYTON *exits.* DIANA *is moved by the excruciating look coming onto Livermore's face.*

DIANA: Mr. Livermore? . . .

ROBERTSON (*entering*): Sorry I'm late, Diana. How was the trip? (*Her expression turns him to* LIVERMORE. *He goes to him.*) Bad, Jesse?

LIVERMORE: I am wiped out, Arthur.

ROBERTSON (*trying for lightness*): Come on, now, Jesse, a man like you has always got ten million put away somewhere.

LIVERMORE: No, no. I always felt that if you couldn't have *real* money, might as well not have any. Is it true what I've heard, that you sold out in time?

ROBERTSON: Yes, Jesse. I told you I would.

LIVERMORE (*slight pause*): Arthur, can you lend me five thousand dollars?

ROBERTSON: Certainly. (*He sits, removes one shoe. To audience:*) Five weeks ago, on his yacht in Oyster Bay, he told me he had four hundred and eighty million dollars in common stocks.

LIVERMORE: What the hell are you doing?

> ROBERTSON *removes a layer of five thousand-dollar bills from the shoe and hands* LIVERMORE *one as he stands.* LIVERMORE *stares down at Robertson's shoes.*

By God. Don't you believe in anything?

ROBERTSON: Not much.

LIVERMORE: Well, I suppose I understand that. (*He folds the bill.*) But I can't say that I admire it. (*He pockets the bill, looks down again at Robertson's shoes, and shakes his head.*) Well, I guess it's your country now. (*He turns like a blind man and goes out.*)

ROBERTSON: Not long after, Jesse Livermore sat down to a good breakfast in the Sherry-Netherland Hotel and, calling for an envelope, addressed it to Arthur Robertson, inserted a note for five thousand dollars, went into the washroom, and shot himself.

DIANA (*staring after* LIVERMORE, *then turning to* ROBERTSON): Is Randolph ruined too?

ROBERTSON (*taking her hand*): Diana . . . Randolph is dead. (*Pause.*) He . . . he fell from his window.

> DIANA *stands, astonished.* IRENE *sings* " 'Tain't Nobody's Bizness" *from choral area. Fadeout.*

ROSE (*calling as she enters*): Lee? Darling?

LEE (*takes a bike from prop area and rides on, halting before her*): How do you like it, Ma!

ROSE: What a beautiful bike!

LEE: It's a Columbia Racer! I just bought it from Georgie Rosen for twelve dollars.

ROSE: Where'd you get twelve dollars?

LEE: I emptied my savings account. But it's worth way more! . . .

ROSE: Well, I should say! Listen, darling, you know how to get to Third Avenue and Nineteenth Street, don't you?

LEE: Sure, in ten minutes.

ROSE (*taking a diamond bracelet from her bag*): This is my diamond bracelet. (*She reaches into the bag and brings out a card.*) And this is Mr. Sanders' card and the address. He's expecting you; just give it to him, and he'll give you a receipt.

LEE: Is he going to fix it?

ROSE: No, dear. It's a pawnshop. Go. I'll explain sometime.

LEE: Can't I have an idea? What's a pawnshop?

ROSE: Where you leave something temporarily and they lend you money on it, with interest. I'm going to leave it the rest of the month, till the market goes up again. I showed it to him on Friday, and we're getting a nice loan on it.

LEE: But how do you get it back?

ROSE: You just pay back the loan plus interest. But things'll pick up in a month or two. Go on, darling, and be careful! I'm so glad you bought that bike. . . . It's gorgeous!

LEE (*mounting his bike*): Does Papa know?

ROSE: Yes, dear. Papa knows . . .

> She starts out as JOEY *hurries on.*

JOEY: Oh, hiya, Mrs. Baum.

ROSE: Hello, Joey. . . . Did you get thin?

JOEY: Me? (*He touches his stomach defensively.*) No, I'm okay. (*To* LEE *as well, as he takes an eight-by-ten photo out of an envelope:*) See what I just got?

> ROSE *and* LEE *look at the photo.*

ROSE (*impressed*): Where did you get that!

LEE: How'd you get it autographed?

JOEY: I just wrote to the White House.

LEE (*running his finger over the signature*): Boy . . . look at that, huh? "Herbert Hoover"!

ROSE: What a human thing for him to do! What did you write him?

JOEY: Just wished him success . . . you know, against the Depression.

ROSE (*wondrously*): Look at that! You're going to end up a politician, Joey. (*She returns to studying the photo.*)

JOEY: I might. I like it a lot.

LEE: But what about dentistry?

JOEY: Well, either one.

ROSE: Get going, darling.

> She exits, already preoccupied with the real problem. LEE mounts his bike.

LEE: You want to shoot some baskets later?

JOEY: What about now?

LEE (*embarrassed*): No . . . I've got something to do for my mother. Meet you on the court in an hour. (*He starts off.*)

JOEY (*stopping him*): Wait, I'll go with you, let me on! (*He starts to mount the crossbar.*)

LEE: I can't, Joey.

JOEY (*sensing some forbidden area, surprised*): Oh!

LEE: See you on the court.

> LEE *rides off.* JOEY *examines the autograph and mouths silently, "Herbert Hoover . . ." He shakes his head proudly and walks off.*

ROBERTSON (*from choral area*): To me . . . it's beginning to look like Germany in 1922, and I'm having real worries about the banks. There are times when I walk around with as much as twenty-five, thirty thousand dollars in my shoes.

> FRANK *enters in a chauffeur's uniform, a lap robe folded over his arm.* MOE *enters, stylishly dressed in a fur-collared over-coat, as though on a street.*

FRANK: Morning, Mr. Baum. Got the car nice and warmed up for you this morning, sir. And I had the lap robe dry-cleaned.

MOE (*showing* FRANK *a bill*): What is that, Frank?

FRANK: Oh. Looks like the garage bill.

MOE: What's that about tires on there?

FRANK: Oh, yes, sir, this is the bill for the new tires last week.

MOE: And what happened to those tires we bought six weeks ago?

FRANK: Those weren't very good, sir, they wore out quick—and I want to be the first to admit that!

MOE: But twenty dollars apiece and they last six weeks?

FRANK: That's just what I'm telling you, sir—they were just no good. But these ones are going to be a whole lot better, though.

MOE: Tell you what, Frank . . .

FRANK: Yes, sir—what I mean, I'm giving you my personal guarantee on this set, Mr. Baum.

MOE: I never paid no attention to these things, but maybe you heard of the market crash? The whole thing practically floated into the ocean, y'know.

FRANK: Oh, yes, sir, I certainly heard about it.

MOE: I'm glad you heard about it, because I heard a *lot* about it. In fact, what you cleared from selling my tires over the last ten years . . .

FRANK: Oh, no, sir! Mr. Baum!

MOE: Frank, lookin' back over the last ten years, I never heard of that amount of tires in my whole life since I first come over from Europe a baby at the age of six. That is a lot of tires, Frank; so I tell ya what we're gonna do now, you're going to drive her over to the Pierce Arrow showroom and leave her there, and then come to my office and we'll settle up.

FRANK: But how are you going to get around!

MOE: I'm a happy man in a taxi, Frank.

FRANK: Well, I'm sure going to be sorry to leave you people.

MOE: Everything comes to an end, Frank, it was great while it lasted. No hard feelings. (*He shakes Frank's hand.*) Bye-bye.

FRANK: But what . . . what am I supposed to do now?

MOE: You got in-laws?

FRANK: But I never got along with them.

MOE: You should've. (*He hurries off, calling:*) Taxi!

FRANK (*cap in hand, throws down lap robe and walks off aimlessly*): Damn!

>   IRENE *enters with a pram filled with junk and sings a few lines of " 'Tain't Nobody's Bizness," unaccompanied. She picks up robe and admiringly inspects it. Then:*

IRENE: You got fired, you walked away to nothing; no unemployment insurance, no Social Security—just the in-laws and fresh air. (*She tosses the robe in with her junk.*)

>   *Fadeout.*

ROSE: Still . . . it was very nice in a certain way. On our block in

Brooklyn a lot of married children had to move back with the parents, and you heard babies crying in houses that didn't have a baby in twenty years. But of course the doubling up could also drive you crazy . . .

With hardly a pause, she turns to GRANDPA, *who is arriving center with canes and hatboxes. He drops the whole load on the floor.*

What are *you* doing?

GRANDPA (*delivering a final verdict*): There's no room for these in my closet . . .

ROSE: For a few *canes*?

GRANDPA: And what about my hats? You shouldn't have bought such a small house, Rose.

ROSE (*of the canes*): I'll put them in the front-hall closet.

GRANDPA: No, people step on them. And where will I put my hats?

ROSE (*trying not to explode*): Papa, what do you want from me? We are doing what we can do!

GRANDPA: One bedroom for so many people is not right! You had three bathrooms in the apartment, and you used to look out the window, there was the whole New York. Here . . . listen to that street out there, it's a Brooklyn cemetery. And this barber here is *very* bad—look what he did to me. (*He shows her.*)

ROSE: Why? It's beautiful. (*She brushes some hairs straight.*) It's just a little uneven . . .

GRANDPA (*pushing her hand away*): I don't understand, Rose— why does he declare bankruptcy if he's going to turn around and pay his debts?

ROSE: For his reputation.

GRANDPA: His reputation! He'll have the reputation of a fool! The reason to go bankrupt is *not* to pay your debts!

ROSE (*uncertain herself*): He wanted to be honorable.

GRANDPA: But that's the whole beauty of it! He should've asked me. When I went bankrupt I didn't pay *nobody*!

ROSE (*deciding*): I've got to tell you something, Papa. From now on, I wish you . . .

GRANDPA (*helping her fold a bed sheet*): And you'll have to talk to Lee—he throws himself around in his bed all night, wakes me up ten times, and he leaves his socks on the floor. . . . Two people in that bedroom is too much, Rose.

ROSE: I don't want Moe to get aggravated, Papa.

He is reached, slightly glances at her.

He might try to start a new business, so he's nervous, so please, don't complain, Papa. Please?

GRANDPA: What did I say?

ROSE: Nothing. (*Suddenly she embraces him guiltily.*) Maybe I can find an umbrella stand someplace.

GRANDPA: I was reading about this Hitler . . .

ROSE: Who?

GRANDPA: . . . He's chasing all the radicals out of Germany. He wouldn't be so bad if he wasn't against the Jews. But he won't last six months. . . . The Germans are not fools. When I used to take Mama to Baden-Baden this time of year . . .

ROSE: How beautiful she was.

GRANDPA: . . . one time we were sitting on the train ready to leave for Berlin. And suddenly a man gallops up calling out my name.

So I says, "Yes, that's me!" And through the window he hands me my gold watch and chain: "You left it in your room, mein Herr." Such a thing could only happen in Germany. This Hitler is finished.

ROSE (*of the canes*): Please. . . . Put them back in your closet, heh? (*He starts to object.*) I don't want Moe to get mad, Papa! (*She cuts the rebellion short and loads him with his canes and hatboxes.*)

GRANDPA (*muttering*): Man don't even know how to go bankrupt.

> *He exits.* LEE *appears on his bike—but dressed now for winter. He dismounts and parks the bike just as* ROSE *lies back in the chair.*

LEE: Ma! Guess what!

ROSE: What?

LEE: Remember I emptied my bank account for the bike?

ROSE: So?

LEE: The bank has just been closed by the government! It's broke! There's a whole mob of people in the street yelling where's their money! They've got cops and everything! There is no more money in the bank!

ROSE: You're a genius!

LEE: Imagine! . . . I could have lost my twelve dollars! . . . Wow!

ROSE: That's wonderful. (*She removes a pearl choker.*)

LEE: Oh, Ma, wasn't that Papa's wedding present?

ROSE: I hate to, but . . .

LEE: What about Papa's business! Can't he . . .

ROSE: He put too much capital in the stock market, dear—it made more there than in his business. So now . . . it's not there anymore.

A THIEF *swiftly appears and rides off on the bike.*

But we'll be all right. Go. You can have a jelly sandwich when you come back.

LEE *stuffs the pearls into his pants as he approaches where the bike was; he looks in all directions, his bones chilling. He runs in all directions and finally comes to a halt, breathless, stark horror in his face. As though sensing trouble,* ROSE *walks over to him.*

Where's your bike?

He can't speak.

They stole your bike?

He is immobile.

May he choke on his next meal. . . . Oh, my darling, my darling, what an awful thing.

He sobs once but holds it back. She, facing him, tries to smile.

So now you're going to have to walk to the hockshop like everybody else. Come, have your jelly sandwich.

LEE: No, I'd like to see if I can trot there—it'd be good for my track. By the way, I've almost decided to go to Cornell, I think. Cornell or Brown.

ROSE (*with an empty congratulatory exclamation*): Oh! . . . Well, there's still months to decide.

ROSE *and* LEE *join the company as they stand up to sing the Iowa Hymn, Verse 1: "We gather together to ask the Lord's blessing, He chastens and hastens His will to make known: The wicked oppressing now cease from distressing, Sing*

*praises to His name: He forgets not His own." The hymn
music continues under the following.*

ROBERTSON: Till then, probably most people didn't think of it as a
system.

TAYLOR: It was more like nature.

MRS. TAYLOR: Like weather; had to expect bad weather, but it
always got good again if you waited. And so we waited. And it
didn't change. (*She is watching* TAYLOR *as he adopts a mood of
despair and slowly sits on his heels.*) And we waited some more
and it never changed. You couldn't hardly believe that the day
would come when the land wouldn't give. Land always gives.
But there it lay, miles and miles of it, and there was us wanting
to work it, and couldn't. It was like a spell on Iowa. We was all
there, and the land was there waitin', and we wasn't able to
move. (*The hymn ends.*) Amen.

BREWSTER, *followed by* FARMERS, *comes front and calls to
the crowd in the audience's direction.*

BREWSTER: Just sit tight, folks, be startin' in a few minutes.

FARMER 1 (*hitting his heels together*): Looks like snow up there.

FARMER 2 (*laughs*): Even the weather ain't workin'.

Low laughter in the crowd.

BREWSTER (*heading over to* TAYLOR): You be catchin' cold sitting
on the ground like that, won't you, Henry?

TAYLOR: Tired out. Never slept a wink all night. Not a wink.

MRS. TAYLOR *appears carrying a big coffeepot, accompanied
by* HARRIET, *her fifteen-year-old daughter, who has a coffee
mug hanging from each of her fingers.*

MRS. TAYLOR: You'll have to share the cups, but it's something hot
anyway.

BREWSTER: Oh, that smells good, lemme take that, ma'am.

> *She gives the coffeepot to* BREWSTER *and comes over to* TAYLOR. HARRIET *hands out the cups.*

MRS. TAYLOR (*sotto voce, irritated and ashamed*): You can't be sitting on the ground like that, now come on! (*She starts him to his feet.*) It's a auction—anybody's got a right to come to a auction.

TAYLOR: There must be a thousand men along the road—they never told me they'd bring a thousand men!

MRS. TAYLOR: Well, I suppose that's the way they do it.

TAYLOR: They got guns in those trucks!

MRS. TAYLOR (*frightened herself*): Well, it's too late to stop 'em now. So might as well go around and talk to people that come to help you.

CHARLEY (*rushing on*): Brewster! Where's Brewster!

BREWSTER (*stepping forward from the crowd*): What's up, Charley?

CHARLEY (*pointing off*): Judge Bradley! He's gettin' out of the car with the auctioneer!

> *Silence. All look to* BREWSTER.

BREWSTER: Well . . . I don't see what that changes. (*Turning to all:*) I guess we're gonna do what we come here to do. That right?

> *The crowd quietly agrees: "Right," "Stick to it, Larry," "No use quittin' now," etc. Enter* JUDGE BRADLEY, *sixty, and* MR. FRANK HOWARD, *the auctioneer. The silence spreads.*

JUDGE BRADLEY: Good morning, gentlemen. (*He looks around. There is no reply.*) I want to say a few words to you before Mr.

Howard starts the auction. (*He walks up onto a raised platform.*) I have decided to come here personally this morning in order to emphasize the gravity of the situation that has developed in the state. We are on the verge of anarchy in Iowa, and that is not going to help anybody. Now, you are all property owners, so you—

BREWSTER: Used to be, Judge, used to be!

JUDGE BRADLEY: Brewster, I will not waste words; there are forty armed deputies out there. (*Slight pause.*) I would like to make only one point clear—I have levied a deficiency judgment on this farm. Mr. Taylor has failed to pay what he owes on his equipment and some of his cattle. A contract is sacred. The National Bank has the right to collect on its loans. Now then, Mr. Howard will begin the auction. But he has discretionary power to decline any unreasonable bid. I ask you again, obey the law. Once law and order go down, no man is safe. Mr. Howard?

MR. HOWARD (*with a clipboard in hand, climbs onto the platform*): Well, now, let's see. We have here one John Deere tractor and combine, three years old, beautiful condition.

> Three BIDDERS *enter, and the crowd turns to look at them with hostility as they come to a halt.*

I ask for bids on the tractor and combine.

BREWSTER: Ten cents!

MR. HOWARD: I have ten cents. (*His finger raised, he points from man to man in the crowd.*) I have ten cents, I have ten cents . . .

> He is pointing toward the BIDDERS, *but they are looking around at the crowd in fear.*

BIDDER 1: Five hundred.

JUDGE BRADLEY (*calling*): Sheriff, get over here and protect these men!

The SHERIFF *and four* DEPUTIES *enter and edge their way in around the three* BIDDERS. *The deputies carry shotguns.*

MR. HOWARD: Do I hear five hundred dollars? Do I hear five . . .

BIDDER 1: Five hundred!

MR. HOWARD: Do I hear six hundred?

BIDDER 2: Six hundred!

MR. HOWARD: Do I hear seven hundred?

BIDDER 3: Seven hundred!

Disciplined and quick, the FARMERS *grab the* DEPUTIES *and disarm them; a shotgun goes off harmlessly.*

JUDGE BRADLEY: Brewster! Great God, what are you doing!

BREWSTER *has pinned the Judge's arms behind him, and another man lowers a noose around his neck.*

BREWSTER (*to* DEPUTIES): You come any closer and we're gonna string him up! You all get back on that road or we string up the Judge! So help me Christ, he goes up if any one of you deputies interferes with this auction! Now, let me just clear up one thing for you, Judge Bradley . . .

TAYLOR: Let him go, Brewster—I don't care anymore, let them take it!

BREWSTER: Just sit tight, Henry, nobody's takin' anything. That is all over, Judge. Mr. Howard, just to save time, why don't you take a bid on the whole place? Do that, please?

MR. HOWARD (*turns to the crowd, his voice shaking*): I . . . I'll hear bids on . . . everything. Tractor and combine, pair of mules and wagon, twenty-six cows, eight heifers, farm and outbuildings, assorted tools . . . and so forth. Do I hear . . .

BREWSTER: One dollar.

MR. HOWARD (*rapidly*): I hear one dollar. One dollar, one dollar? . . . (*He looks around.*) Sold for one dollar.

BREWSTER (*handing him a dollar*): Now, will you just sign that receipt, please?

> MR. HOWARD *scribbles and hands him a receipt.* BREWSTER *leaps off the platform, goes to* TAYLOR, *and gives him the receipt.*

Henry? Whyn't you go along now and get to milkin'. Let's go, boys.

> *He waves to the crowd, and his men follow him out.* JUDGE BRADLEY, *removing the noose, comes down off the platform and goes over to* TAYLOR, *who is staring down at the receipt.*

JUDGE BRADLEY: Henry Taylor? You are nothing but a thief!

> TAYLOR *cringes under the accusation. The* JUDGE *points to the receipt.*

That is a crime against every law of God and man! And this isn't the end of it, either! (*He turns and stalks out.*)

HARRIET: Should we milk 'em, Papa?

MRS. TAYLOR: Of course we milk 'em—they're ours. (*But she needs Taylor's compliance.*) Henry?

TAYLOR (*staring at the receipt*): It's like I stole my own place.

> *Near tears, humiliated,* TAYLOR *moves into darkness with his wife. The* FARMERS *disperse.*

ROBERTSON (*from choral area*): Nobody knows how many people are leaving their hometowns, their farms and cities, and hitting the road. Hundreds of thousands, maybe millions of internal refugees, Americans transformed into strangers.

> BANKS *enters in army cap, uniform jacket and jeans, carrying his little bundle of clothes and a cooking pot.*

BANKS:

> I still hear that train.
> Still hear that long low whistle.
> Still hear that train, yeah.

He imitates train whistle: Whoo-ooo! *He sings the first verse of "How Long," then speaks over music, which continues.*

Nineteen twenty-nine was pretty hard. My family had a little old cotton farm, McGehee, Arkansas. But a man had to be on the road—leave his wife, his mother—just to try to get a little money to live on. But God help me, I couldn't get anything, and I was too ashamed to send them a picture, all dirty and ragged and hadn't shaved. Write a postcard: "Dear Mother, doin' wonderful and hope you're all fine." And me sleepin' on a Los Angeles sidewalk under a newspaper. And my ma'd say, "Oh, my son's in Los Angeles, he's doin' pretty fair." (*He grins.*) Yeah . . . "all the way on the Santa Fe." So hungry and weak I begin to see snakes through the smoke, and a white hobo named Callahan got a scissors on me, wrapped me 'tween his legs—otherwise I'd have fell off into a cornfield there. But except for Callahan there was no friendships in the hobo jungle. Everybody else was worried and sad-lookin', and they was evil to each other. I still hear that long low whistle . . . *whoo-ooo!*

BANKS sings the second verse of "How Long." Then the music changes into "The Joint is Jumpin' ": MARATHON DANCERS *enter, half asleep, some about to drop. They dance. Fadeout.*

Light comes up on MOE *in an armchair.* LEE *enters with college catalogues.*

MOE: When you say three hundred dollars tuition . . . Lee!

LEE: That's for Columbia. Some of these others are cheaper.

MOE: That's for the four years.

LEE: Well, no, that's one year.

MOE: Ah. (*He lies back in the chair and closes his eyes.*)

LEE (*flipping a page of a catalogue*): Minnesota here is a hundred and fifty, for instance. And Ohio State is about the same, I think. (*He turns to* MOE, *awaiting his reaction.*) Pa?

   MOE *is asleep.*

He always got drowsy when the news got bad. And now the mystery of the marked house began. Practically every day you'd see the stranger coming down the street, poor and ragged, and he'd go past house after house, but at our driveway he'd make a turn right up to the back porch and ask for something to eat. Why us?

   TAYLOR *appears at one side of the stage in mackinaw, farm shoes, and peaked hunter's cap, a creased paper bag under his arm. Looking front, he seems gaunt, out of his element; now he rings the doorbell. Nothing happens. Then* LEE *goes to the "door."*

LEE: Yes?

TAYLOR (*shyly, still an amateur at the routine*): Ah . . . sorry to be botherin' you on a Sunday and all.

ROSE (*enters in housedress and apron, wiping her hands on a dish towel*): Who is that, dear? (*She comes to the door.*)

LEE: This is my mother.

TAYLOR: How-de-do, ma'am, my name is Taylor, and I'm just passing by, wondering if you folks have any work around the place . . .

MOE (*waking up suddenly*): Hey! The bell rang! (*He sees the conclave.*) Oh . . .

ROSE (*ironically*): Another one looking for work!

TAYLOR: I could paint the place or fix the roof, electrical, plumbing, masonry, gardening . . . I always had my own farm, and we do all that, don't you know. I'd work cheap . . .

ROSE: Well, we don't need any kind of . . .

MOE: Where you from?

TAYLOR: State of Iowa.

LEE (*as though it's the moon*): Iowa!

TAYLOR: I wouldn't hardly charge if I could have my meals, don't you know.

MOE (*beginning to locate* TAYLOR *in space*): Whereabouts in Iowa?

ROSE: My sister's husband comes from Cleveland.

MOE: No, no, Cleveland is nowhere near. (*To* TAYLOR:) Whereabouts?

TAYLOR: You know Styles?

MOE: I only know the stores in the big towns.

TAYLOR (*giving a grateful chuckle*): Well! I never expected to meet a . . .

>   *He suddenly gets dizzy, breaks off, and reaches for some support.* LEE *holds his arm, and he goes down like an elevator and sits there.*

ROSE: What's the matter!

MOE: Mister?

LEE: I'll get water! (*He rushes out.*)

ROSE: Is it your heart?

TAYLOR: 'Scuse me . . . I'm awful sorry . . .

>   *He gets on his hands and knees as* LEE *enters with a glass of water and hands it to him. He drinks half of it, returns the glass.*

Thank you, sonny.

ROSE (*looks to* MOE, *sees his agreement, gestures within*): He better sit down.

MOE: You want to sit down?

> TAYLOR *looks at him helplessly.*

Come, sit down.

> LEE *and* MOE *help him to a chair, and he sits.*

ROSE (*bending over to look into his face*): You got some kind of heart?

TAYLOR (*embarrassed, and afraid for himself now*): Would you be able to give me something to eat?

> *The three stare at him; he looks up at their shocked astonishment and weeps.*

ROSE: You're *hungry*?

TAYLOR: Yes, ma'am.

> ROSE *looks at* MOE *whether to believe this.*

MOE (*unnerved*): Better get him something.

ROSE (*hurrying out immediately*): Oh, my God in heaven!

MOE (*now with a suspicious, even accusatory edge*): What're you doing, just going around? . . .

TAYLOR: Well, no, I come east when I lost the farm. . . . They was supposed to be hiring in New Jersey, pickers for the celery? But I only got two days. . . . I been to the Salvation Army four, five times, but they only give me a bun and a cup of coffee yesterday . . .

LEE: You haven't eaten since *yesterday*?

TAYLOR: Well, I generally don't need too much . . .

ROSE (*entering with a tray, bowl of soup, and bread*): I was just making it, so I didn't put in the potatoes yet . . .

TAYLOR: Oh, beets?

ROSE: That's what you call borscht.

TAYLOR (*obediently*): Yes, ma'am.

> *He wastes no time, spoons it up. They all watch him: their first hungry man.*

MOE (*skeptically*): How do you come to lose a farm?

TAYLOR: I suppose you read about the Farmers' Uprisin' in the state couple months ago?

LEE: I did.

MOE (*to* LEE): What uprising?

LEE: They nearly lynched a judge for auctioning off their farms. (*To* TAYLOR, *impressed:*) Were you in *that*?

TAYLOR: Well, it's all over now, but I don't believe they'll be auctioning any more farms for a while, though. Been just terrible out there.

ROSE (*shaking her head*): And I thought they were all Republicans in Iowa.

TAYLOR: Well, I guess they all are.

LEE: Is that what they mean by radical, though?

TAYLOR: Well . . . it's like they say—people in Iowa are practical. They'll even go radical if it seems like it's practical. But as soon as it stops being practical they stop being radical.

MOE: Well, you probably all learned your lesson now.

LEE: Why! He was taking their homes away, that judge!

MOE: So you go in a court and lynch him?

LEE: But . . . but it's all *wrong*, Pa!

ROSE: Shh! Don't argue . . .

LEE (*to* ROSE): But *you* think it's wrong, don't you? Suppose they came and threw us out of *this* house?

ROSE: I refuse to think about it. (*To* TAYLOR:) So where do you sleep?

MOE (*instantly*): Excuse me. We are not interested in where you sleep, Mr. . . . what's your name?

TAYLOR: Taylor. I'd be satisfied with just my meals if I could live in the basement . . .

MOE (*to* TAYLOR, *but half addressing* ROSE): There is no room for another human being in this house, y'understand? Including the basement. (*He takes out two or three bills.*)

TAYLOR: I wasn't asking for charity . . .

MOE: I'm going to loan you a dollar, and I hope you're going to start a whole new life. Here . . . (*He hands* TAYLOR *the bill, escorting him to the door.*) And pay me back, but don't rush. (*He holds out his hand.*) Glad to have met you, and good luck.

TAYLOR: Thanks for the soup, Mrs. . . .

ROSE: Our name is Baum. You have children?

TAYLOR: One's fifteen, one's nine. (*He thoughtfully folds the dollar bill.*)

GRANDPA *enters, eating a plum.*

ROSE: Take care of yourself, and write a letter to your wife.

TAYLOR: Yes, I will. (*To* MOE:) Goodbye, sir . . .

MOE (*grinning, tipping his finger at* TAYLOR): Stay away from rope.

TAYLOR: Oh, yeah, I will . . . (*He exits.*)

LEE (*goes out on the periphery and calls to him as he walks away*): Goodbye, Mr. Taylor!

TAYLOR (*turns back, waves*): Bye, sonny!

He leaves. LEE *stares after him, absorbing it all.*

GRANDPA: Who was that?

MOE: He's a farmer from Iowa. He tried to lynch a judge, so she wanted him to live in the cellar.

GRANDPA: What is a farmer doing here?

ROSE: He went broke, he lost everything.

GRANDPA: Oh. Well, he should borrow.

MOE (*snaps his fingers to* LEE): I'll run down the street and tell him! He got me hungry. (*To* ROSE:) I'm going down the corner and get a chocolate soda. . . . What do you say, Lee?

LEE: I don't feel like it.

MOE: Don't be sad. Life is tough, what're you going to do? Sometimes it's not as tough as other times, that's all. But it's always tough. Come, have a soda.

LEE: Not now, Pa, thanks. (*He turns away.*)

MOE (*straightens, silently refusing blame*): Be back right away. (*He strolls across the stage, softly, tonelessly whistling, and exits.*)

   GRANDPA, *chewing, the plum pit in his hand, looks around for a place to put it.* ROSE *sees the inevitable and holds out her hand.*

ROSE (*disgusted*): Oh, give it to me.

   GRANDPA *drops the pit into her palm, and she goes out with it and the soup plate.*

LEE (*still trying to digest*): That man was starving, Grandpa.

GRANDPA: No, no, he was hungry but not starving.

LEE: He was, he almost fainted.

GRANDPA: No, that's not starving. In Europe they starve, but here not. Anyway, couple weeks they're going to figure out what to do, and you can forget the whole thing. . . . God makes one person at a time, boy—worry about yourself.

Fadeout.

ROBERTSON: His name is Theodore K. Quinn.

Music begins—"My Baby Just Cares for Me"—and QUINN, *with boater and cane, sings and dances through Robertson's speech.*

The greatest Irish soft-shoe dancer ever to serve on a board of directors. They know him at Lindy's, they love him at Twenty-one. High up on top of the American heap sits Ted Quinn, hardly forty years of age in 1932 . . .

QUINN (*continues singing, then breaks off and picks up the phone*): Ted Quinn. Come over, Arthur, I've got to see you. But come to the twenty-ninth floor. . . . I've got a new office.

ROBERTSON (*looking around, as at a striking office*): All this yours?

QUINN: Yup. You are standing on the apex, the pinnacle of human evolution. From that window you can reach out and touch the moustache of Almighty God.

ROBERTSON (*moved, gripping Quinn's hand*): Ted! *Ted!!*

QUINN: Jesus, don't say it that way, will ya?

ROBERTSON: President of General Electric!

QUINN: I'm not sure I want it, Arthur.

ROBERTSON *laughs sarcastically.*

I'm not, goddammit! I never expected Swope to pick me— never!

ROBERTSON: Oh, go on, you've been angling for the presidency the last five years.

QUINN: No! I swear not. I just didn't want anybody else to get it . . .

ROBERTSON *laughs*.

Well, that's not the same thing! . . . Seriously, Arthur, I'm scared. I don't know what to do. (*He looks around.*) Now that I'm standing here, now that they're about to paint my name on the door . . . and the *Times* sending a reporter . . .

ROBERTSON (*seriously*): What the hell's got into you?

QUINN (*searching in himself*): I don't know. . . . It's almost like shame.

ROBERTSON: For *what*? It's that damned upbringing of yours, that anarchist father . . .

QUINN: The truth is, I've never been comfortable with some of the things we've done.

ROBERTSON: But why suddenly after all these years . . .

QUINN: It's different taking orders and being the man who gives them.

ROBERTSON: I don't know what the hell you are talking about.

Pause. For QUINN *it is both a confession and something he* must *bring out into the open. But he sustains his humor.*

QUINN: I had a very unsettling experience about eighteen months ago, Arthur. Got a call from my Philadelphia district manager that Frigidaire was dropping the price on their boxes. So I told him to cut ours. And in a matter of weeks they cut, we cut, they cut, we cut, till I finally went down there myself. Because I was damned if I was going to get beat in Philadelphia . . . and I finally cut our price right down to our cost of production. Well—ting-a-ling-a-ling, phone call from New York: "What the hell is going on down there?" Gotta get down to Wall Street and have a meeting with the money boys. . . . So there we are, about ten of us, and I look across the blinding glare of that teakwood table, and lo and behold, who is facing me but Georgy Fairchild, head of sales for Frigidaire. Old friends, Georgy and I, go way back together, but he *is* Frigidaire, y'know—what the hell is he doing in a GE meeting? . . . Well, turns out that both companies are owned by the same money. And the word is that Georgy and Quinn are going to cut out this nonsense and get those prices up to where they belong. (*He laughs.*) Well, I tell you, I was absolutely flabbergasted. Here I've been fightin' Georgy from Bangkok to the Bronx, layin' awake nights thinkin' how to outfox him—hell, we were like Grant and Lee with thousands of soldiers out to destroy each other, and it's suddenly like all these years I'd been shellin' my own men! (*He laughs.*) It was farcical.

ROBERTSON: It's amazing. You're probably the world's greatest salesman, and you haven't an ounce of objectivity . . .

QUINN: Objectivity! Arthur, if I'm that great a salesman—which I'm far from denying—it's because I believe; I believe deeply in the creative force of competition.

ROBERTSON: Exactly, and GE is the fastest-growing company in the world because . . .

QUINN (loves *this point*): . . . because we've had the capital to buy up one independent business after another. . . . It's haunting me, Arthur—thousands of small businesses are going under every week now, and we're getting bigger and bigger every day. What's going to become of the independent person in this country once everybody's sucking off the same tit? How can there be an America without Americans—people not beholden to some enormous enterprise that'll run their souls?

ROBERTSON: Am I hearing what I think?

QUINN *is silent.*

Ted? You'd actually resign?

QUINN: If I did, would it make any point to you at all? If I made a statement that . . .

ROBERTSON: What statement can you possibly make that won't call for a return to the horse and buggy? The America you love is cold stone dead in the parlor, Ted. This is a corporate country; you can't go back to small personal enterprise again.

QUINN: A corporate country! . . . Jesus, Arthur, what a prospect!

MISS FOWLER *enters.*

MISS FOWLER: The gentleman from the *Times* is waiting, Mr. Quinn . . . unless you'd like to make it tomorrow or . . .

QUINN (*slight pause*): No, no—it has to be now or never. Ask him in.

She exits.

Tell me the truth, Arthur, do I move your mind at all?

ROBERTSON: Of course I see your point. But you can't buck the inevitable.

GRAHAM *enters with* MISS FOWLER.

MISS FOWLER: Mr. Graham.

QUINN (*shakes hands, grinning*): Glad to meet you. . . . My friend Mr. Robertson.

GRAHAM (*recognizing the name*): Oh, yes, how do you do?

ROBERTSON: Nice to meet you. (*To* QUINN, *escaping:*) I'll see you later . . .

QUINN: No, stay . . . I'll only be a few minutes . . .

ROBERTSON: I ought to get back to my office.

QUINN (*laughs*): I'm still the president, Arthur—stay! I want to feel the support of your opposition.

> ROBERTSON *laughs with* QUINN, *glancing uneasily at* GRAHAM, *who doesn't know what's going on.*

I'll have to be quick, Mr. Graham. Will you sit down?

GRAHAM: I have a few questions about your earlier life and background. I understand your father was one of the early labor organizers in Chicago.

QUINN: Mr. Graham, I am resigning.

GRAHAM: Beg your pardon?

QUINN: Resigning, I said.

GRAHAM: From the presidency? I don't understand.

QUINN: I don't believe in giant business, or giant government, or giant anything. And the laugh is . . . no man has done more to make GE the giant it is today.

GRAHAM: Well, now! (*He laughs.*) I think this takes us off the financial section and onto the front page! But tell me, how does a man with your ideas rise so high in a great corporation like this? How did you get into GE?

QUINN: Well, it's a long story, but I love to tell it. I started out studying law at night and working as a clerk in a factory that manufactured bulbs for auto headlights. Y'see, in those days they had forty or fifty makes of car and all different specifications for the lightbulbs. Now, say you got an order for five thousand lamps. The manufacturing process was not too accurate, so you had to make eight or nine thousand to come out with five thousand perfect ones. Result, though, was that we had hundreds of thousands of perfectly good lamps left over at the end of the year. So . . . one night on my own time I went through the records and did some simple calculations and came up with a new average. My figure showed that to get five thousand good bulbs we only had to make sixty-two hundred instead of eight thousand. Result was, that company saved a hundred and thirty thousand dollars in one year. So the boss and I became very friendly, and one day he says, "I'm selling out to General Electric," but he couldn't tell whether they'd be keeping me on. So he says to me, "Ted, tell you what we do. They're coming out from Wall Street"—these bankers, y'see—"and I'm going to let you pick them up at the depot." Figuring I'd be the first to meet them and might draw their attention and they'd rehire me, y'see. Well, I was just this hick-town kid, y'know, about to meet these great big juicy Wall Street bankers—I tell you, I hardly slept all night tryin' to figure how to make an impression. And just toward dawn . . . it was during breakfast—and I suddenly thought of that wall. See, the factory had this brick wall a block long; no windows, two stories high, just a tremendous wall of bricks. And it went through my mind that one of them might ask me how many bricks were in that wall. 'Cause I could answer any question about the company except that. So I got over to the plant as quick as I could, multiplied the vertical and horizontal bricks, and got the number. Well . . . these three bankers arrive, and I get them into the boss's limousine, and we ride. Nobody asks me anything! Three of them in those big fur-lined coats, and not one goddamn syllable. . . . Anyway, we round the corner, and doesn't one of them turn to me and say, "Mr. Quinn, how many bricks you suppose is in that wall!" And by God, I told him! Well, he wouldn't believe it, got out and counted himself—and it broke the ice, y'see, and one thing and another they made me manager of the plant. And that's how I got into GE.

GRAHAM (*astonished*): What are your plans? Will you join another company or . . .

QUINN: No. I've been tickling the idea I might set up an advisory service for small business. Say a fella has a concept, I could teach him how to develop and market it . . . 'cause I *know* all that, and maybe I could help (*to the audience*) to keep those individuals coming. Because with this terrible Depression you hear it everywhere now—an individual man is not worth a bag of peanuts. I don't know the answers, Mr. Graham, but I sure as hell know the question: How do you keep everything that's big from swallowing everything that's small? 'Cause when that happens—God Almighty—it's not going to be much fun!

GRAHAM: Well . . . thanks very much. Good day. Good day, Mr. Robertson. I must say . . .! (*With a broken laugh and a shake of the head, he hurries out.*)

QUINN: He was not massively overwhelmed, was he?

ROBERTSON: He heard the gentle clip-clop of the horse and buggy coming down the road.

QUINN: All right, then, damn it, maybe what you ought to be looking into, Arthur, is horseshoes!

ROBERTSON: Well, you never did do things in a small way! This is unquestionably the world record for the shortest presidency in corporate history. (*He exits.*)

> Alone, QUINN *stares around in a moment of surprise and fright at what he's actually done. Soft-shoe music steals up, and he insinuates himself into it, dancing in a kind of uncertain mood that changes to release and joy, and at the climax he sings the last lines of "My Baby Just Cares for Me." As the lyrics end, the phone rings. He picks up the receiver, never losing the beat, and simply lets it drop, and dances off.*

> ROSE *comes downstage, staring front, a book in her hand.*

ROSE: Who would believe it? You look out the window in the middle of a fine October day, and there's a dozen college graduates with advanced degrees playing ball in the street like children. And it gets harder and harder to remember when life seemed to have so much purpose, when you couldn't wait for the morning!

LEE *enters, takes a college catalogue off the prop table, and approaches her, turning the pages.*

LEE: At Cornell there's no tuition fee at all if you enroll in bacteriology.

ROSE: Free *tuition*!

LEE: Maybe they're short of bacteriologists.

ROSE: Would you like that?

LEE (*stares, tries to see himself as a bacteriologist, sighs*): Bacteriology?

ROSE (*wrinkling her nose*): Must be awful. Is anything else free?

LEE: It's the only one I've seen.

ROSE: I've got to finish this before tomorrow. I'm overdue fourteen cents on it.

LEE: What is it?

ROSE: *Coronet* by Manuel Komroff. It's about this royal crown that gets stolen and lost and found again and lost again for generations. It's supposed to be literature, but I don't know, it's very enjoyable. (*She goes back to her book.*)

LEE (*closes the catalogue, looks at her*): Ma?

ROSE (*still reading*): Hm?

LEE (*gently breaking the ice*): I guess it's too late to apply for this year anyway. Don't you think so?

ROSE (*turns to him*): I imagine so, dear . . . for this year.

LEE: Okay, Ma . . .

ROSE: I feel so terrible—all those years we were throwing money around, and now when you need it—

LEE (*relieved, now that he knows*): That's okay. I think maybe I'll try looking for a job. But I'm not sure whether to look under "Help Wanted, Male" or "Boy Wanted."

ROSE: Boy! (*Their gazes meet. She sees his apprehension.*) Don't be frightened, darling—you're going to be wonderful! (*She hides her feeling in the book.*)

> *Fadeout. Light comes up on* FANNY, *standing on the first-level balcony. She calls to* SIDNEY, *who is playing the piano and singing "Once in a While."*

FANNY: Sidney?

> *He continues singing.*

Sidney?

> *He continues singing.*

Sidney?

> *He continues singing.*

I have to talk to you, Sidney.

> *He continues singing.*

Stop that for a minute!

SIDNEY (*stops singing*): Ma, look . . . it's only July. If I was still in high school it would still be my summer vacation.

FANNY: And if I was the Queen of Rumania I would have free rent. You graduated, Sidney, this is not summer vacation.

SIDNEY: Mama, it's useless to go to employment agencies—there's grown men there, engineers, college graduates. They're willing to take anything. If I could write one hit song like this, just one—we wouldn't have to worry again. Let me have July, just July—see if I can do it. Because that man was serious—he's a good friend of the waiter who works where Bing Crosby's manager eats. He could give him any song I write, and if Crosby just sang it one time . . .

FANNY: I want to talk to you about Doris.

SIDNEY: What Doris?

FANNY: Doris! Doris from downstairs. I've been talking to her mother. She likes you, Sidney.

SIDNEY: Who?

FANNY: Her mother! Mrs. Gross. She's crazy about you.

SIDNEY (*not comprehending*): Oh.

FANNY: She says all Doris does is talk about you.

SIDNEY (*worried*): What is she talking about me for?

FANNY: No, nice things. She likes you.

SIDNEY (*amused, laughs incredulously*): Doris? She's thirteen.

FANNY: She'll be fourteen in December. Now listen to me.

SIDNEY: What, Ma?

FANNY: It's all up to you, Sidney, I want you to make up your own mind. But Papa's never going to get off his back again, and after Lucille's wedding we can forget about *her* salary. Mrs. Gross says—being she's a widow, y'know? And with her goiter and everything . . .

SIDNEY: What?

FANNY: If you like Doris—only if you like her—and you would agree to get married—when she's eighteen, about, or seventeen, even—if you would agree to it now, we could have this apartment rent-free. Starting next month.

SIDNEY (*impressed, even astounded*): Forever?

FANNY: Of course. You would be the husband, it would be your house. You'd move downstairs, with that grand piano and the tile shower . . . I even think if you'd agree she'd throw in the three months' back rent that we owe. I wouldn't even be surprised you could take over the bakery.

SIDNEY: The bakery! For God's sake, Mama, I'm a composer!

FANNY: Now listen to me . . .

DORIS *enters and sits on the floor weaving a cat's cradle of string.*

SIDNEY: But how can I be a baker!

FANNY: Sidney, dear, did you ever once look at that girl?

SIDNEY: Why should I look at her!

FANNY (*taking him to the "window"*): Because she's a beauty. I wouldn't have mentioned it otherwise. Look. Look at that nose. Look at her hands. You see those beautiful little white hands? You don't find hands like that everywhere.

SIDNEY: But Ma, listen—if you just leave me alone for July, and if I write one hit song . . . I know I can do it, Mama.

FANNY: Okay. Sidney, we're behind a hundred and eighty dollars. August first we're out on the street. So write a hit, dear. I only hope that four, five years from now you don't accidentally run into Doris Gross somewhere and fall in love with her—after we all died from exposure!

SIDNEY: But Ma, even if I agreed—supposing next year or the year after I meet some other girl and I really like her . . .

FANNY: All right, and supposing you marry *that* girl and a year after you meet another girl you like better—what are you going to do, get married every year? . . . But I only wanted you to know the situation. I'll close the door, everything'll be quiet. Write a big hit, Sidney! (*She exits.*)

SIDNEY *begins to sing "Once in a While"; *DORIS *echoes him timorously. They trade a few lines,* SIDNEY *hesitant and surprised. Then:*

DORIS (*fully confident, ending the song*): ". . . nearest your heart."

SIDNEY (*sits on his heels beside her as she weaves the string*): Gee, you're really terrific at that, Doris.

He stands, she stands, and they shyly walk off together as he slips his hand into hers.

ROBERTSON (*from choral area*): I guess the most shocking thing is what I see from the window of my Riverside Drive apartment. It's Calcutta on the Hudson, thousands of people living in cardboard boxes right next to that beautiful drive. It is like an army encampment down the length of Manhattan Island. At night you see their campfires flickering, and some nights I go down and walk among them. Remarkable, the humor they still have, but of course people still blame themselves rather than the government. But there's never been a society that hasn't had a clock running on it, and you can't help wondering—how long? How long will they stand for this? So now Roosevelt's got in I'm thinking—boy, he'd better move. He'd better move fast. . . . And you can't help it; first thing every night when I get home, I go to the window and look down at those fires, the flames reflecting off the river through the night.

Lights come up on MOE *and* ROSE. MOE, *in a business suit and hat, is just giving her a peck.*

ROSE: Goodbye, darling. This is going to be a good day—I know it!

MOE (*without much conviction*): I think you're right. G'bye. (*He walks, gradually comes to a halt. Much uncertainty and tension as he glances back toward his house and then looks down to think.*)

LEE *enters, and* ROSE *gives him a farewell kiss. He wears a mackinaw. She hands him a lunch bag.*

ROSE: Don't squeeze it, I put in some cookies. . . . And listen—it doesn't mean you can *never* go to college.

LEE: Oh, I don't mind, Ma. Anyway, I like it around machines. I'm lucky I got the job!

ROSE: All the years we had so much, and now when you need it—

LEE (*cutting her off*): See ya!

> *He leaves her; she exits. He walks and is startled by* MOE *standing there.*

I thought you left a long time ago!

MOE: I'll walk you a way.

> *He doesn't bother explaining, simply walks beside* LEE, *but at a much slower pace than* LEE *took before.* LEE *feels his unusual tension but can only glance over at him with growing apprehension and puzzlement. Finally* MOE *speaks.*

Good job?

LEE: It's okay. I couldn't believe they picked me!

MOE (*nodding*): Good.

> *They walk on in silence, weaving all over the stage, the tension growing as* LEE *keeps glancing at* MOE, *who continuously stares down and ahead as they proceed. At last* MOE *halts and takes a deep breath.*

How much money've you got, Lee?

LEE (*completely taken aback*): . . . money have I got?

MOE (*indicating Lee's pockets*): I mean right now.

LEE: Oh! Well, about . . . (*he takes out change*) . . . thirty-five cents. I'm okay.

MOE: . . . Could I have a quarter? . . . So I can get downtown.

LEE (*pauses an instant, astonished*): Oh, sure, Pa! (*He quickly searches his pockets again.*)

MOE: You got your lunch—I'll need a hotdog later.

LEE (*handing him a quarter*): It's okay. I have a dollar in my drawer. . . . Should I . . . (*He starts to go back.*)

MOE: No, don't go back. (*He proceeds to walk again.*) Don't, ah . . . mention it, heh?

LEE: Oh, no!

MOE: She worries.

LEE: I know. (*To audience:*) We went down to the subway together, and it was hard to look at one another. So we pretended that nothing had happened. (*They come to a halt and sit, as though on a subway.*) But something had. . . . It was like I'd started to support my *father*! And why that should have made me feel so happy, I don't know, but it did! And to cheer him up I began to talk, and before I knew it I was inventing a fantastic future! I said I'd be going to college in no more than a year, at most two; and that I'd straighten out my mind and become an A student; and then I'd not only get a job on a newspaper, but I'd have my own column, no less! By the time we got to Forty-second Street, the Depression was practically over! (*He laughs.*) And in a funny way it *was*— (*He touches his breast*) —in here . . . even though I knew we had a long bad time ahead of us. And so, like most people, I waited with that crazy kind of expectation that comes when there is no hope, waited for the dream to come back from wherever it had gone to hide.

A voice from the theatre sings the end of *"In New York City, You Really Got to Know Your Line,"* or similar song.

END OF ACT ONE

ACT TWO

Rose, *at the piano, has her hands suspended over the keyboard as the band pianist plays. She starts singing "He Loves and She Loves," then breaks off.*

Rose: But this piano is not leaving this house. Jewelry, yes, but nobody hocks this dear, darling piano. (*She "plays" and sings more of the song.*) The crazy ideas people get. Mr. Warsaw on our block, to make a little money he started a racetrack in his kitchen, with cockroaches. Keeps them in matchboxes with their names written on—Alvin, Murray, Irving . . . They bet nickels, dimes. (*She picks up some sheet music.*) Oh, what a show, that *Funny Face.* (*She sings the opening of "S' Wonderful."*) The years go by and you don't get to see a show and Brooklyn drifts further and further into the Atlantic; Manhattan becomes a foreign country, and a year can go by without ever going there. (*She sings more of "S' Wonderful."*) Wherever you look there's a contest; Kellogg's, Post Toasties, win five thousand, win ten thousand. I guess I ought to try, but the winners are always in Indiana somehow. I only pray to God our health holds up, because one filling and you've got to lower the thermostat for a month. Sing! (*She sings the opening of "Do-Do-Do What You Done-Done-Done Before."*) I must go to the library—I must start taking out some good books again; I must stop getting so stupid. I don't see anything, I don't hear anything except money, money, money . . . (*She "plays" Schumann. Fadeout.*)

Robertson (*from choral area*): Looking back, of course, you can see there were two sides to it—with the banks foreclosing right and left, I picked up some first-class properties for a song. I made more money in the thirties than ever before, or since. But I knew a generation was coming of age who would never feel this sense of opportunity.

157

LEE: After a lot of jobs and saving, I did get to the university, and it was a quiet island in the stream. Two pairs of socks and a shirt, plus a good shirt and a mackinaw, and maybe a part-time job in the library, and you could live like a king and never see cash. So there was a distinct reluctance to graduate into that world out there . . . where you knew nobody wanted you.

JOE, RALPH, *and* RUDY *gather in graduation caps and gowns.*

Joey! Is it possible?

JOE: What?

LEE: You're a dentist!

RALPH: Well, I hope things are better when you get out, Lee.

LEE: You decide what to do?

RALPH: There's supposed to be a small aircraft plant still working in Louisville . . .

LEE: Too bad you picked propellers for a specialty.

RALPH: Oh, they'll make airplanes again—soon as there's a war.

LEE: How could there be another war?

JOE: Long as there's capitalism, baby.

RALPH: There'll always be war, y'know, according to the Bible. But if not, I'll probably go into the ministry.

LEE: I never knew you were religious.

RALPH: I'm sort of religious. They pay pretty good, you know, and you get your house and a clothing allowance . . .

JOE (*comes to* LEE, *extending his hand in farewell*): Don't forget to read Karl Marx, Lee. And if you're ever in the neighborhood with a toothache, look me up. I'll keep an eye out for your by-line.

LEE: Oh, I don't expect a newspaper job—papers are closing all over the place. Drop me a card if you open an office.

JOE: It'll probably be in my girl's father's basement. He promised to dig the floor out deeper so I can stand up . . .

LEE: What about equipment?

JOE: I figure two, three years I'll be able to open, if I can make a down payment on a used drill. Come by, I'll put back those teeth Ohio State knocked out.

LEE: I sure will! . . . So long, Rudy!

RUDY: Oh, you might still be seeing me around next semester.

JOE: You staying on campus?

RUDY: I might for the sake of my root canals. If I just take one university course I'm still entitled to the Health Service—could get my canals finished.

LEE: You mean there's a course in the Lit School you haven't taken?

RUDY: Yeah, I just found out about it. Roman Band Instruments.

JOE (*laughs*): You're kiddin'!

RUDY: No, in the Classics Department. Roman Band Instruments. (*He pulls his cheek back.*) See, I've still got three big ones to go on this side.

Laughter.

Well, if you really face it, where am I running? Chicago's loaded with anthropologists. Here, the university's like my mother— I've got free rent, wash dishes for my meals, get my teeth fixed, and God knows, I might pick up the paper one morning and there's an ad: "Help Wanted: Handsome young college graduate, good teeth, must be thoroughly acquainted with Roman band instruments"!

Laughter. They sing "Love and a Dime" accompanied by Rudy on banjo.

RALPH: I'll keep looking for your by-line anyway, Lee.

LEE: No, I doubt it; but I might angle a job on a Mississippi paddleboat when I get out.

RUDY: They still run those?

LEE: Yeah, there's a few. I'd like to retrace Mark Twain's voyages.

RUDY: Well, if you run into Huckleberry Finn—

LEE: I'll give him your regards.

Laughing, RALPH *and* RUDY *start out.*

RALPH: Beat Ohio State, kid!

JOE (*alone with* LEE, *gives him a clenched-fist salute*): So long, Lee.

LEE (*returning the salute*): So long, Joe! (*With fist still clenched, he mimes pulling a whistle, dreamily imagining the Mississippi.*) Toot! Toot!

He moves to a point, taking off his shirt, with which he wipes sweat off his face and neck as in the distance we hear a paddleboat's engines and wheel in water and whistle. LEE *stares out as though from a deck. He is seeing aloud.*

How scary and beautiful the Mississippi is. How do they manage to live? Every town has a bank boarded up, and all those skinny men sitting on the sidewalks with their backs against the storefronts. It's all stopped; like a magic spell. And the anger, the anger . . . when they were handing out meat and beans to the hungry, and the maggots wriggling out of the beef, and that man pointing his rifle at the butcher demanding the fresh meat the government had paid him to hand out . . . How could this have happened, is Marx right? Paper says twelve executives in tobacco made more than thirty thousand farmers who raised it. How long can they accept this? The anger has a smell, it hangs in the air wherever people gather. . . . Fights suddenly break out and simmer down. Is this when revolution comes? And why not? How would Mark Twain write what I have seen? Armed deputies guarding cornfields and whole families sitting beside the road, staring at that food which nobody can buy and is rotting on the stalk. It's insane. (*He exits.*)

ROSE (*from choral area, to audience*): But how can he become a sportswriter if he's a Communist?

> JOE, *carrying a large basket of flowers, crosses downstage to the sound effect of a subway train passing. He sings a verse of "In New York City, You Really Got to Know Your Line." He then breaks upstage and enters Isabel's apartment. She is in bed.*

ISABEL: Hello, honey.

JOE: Could you start calling me Joe? It's less anonymous. (*He starts removing his shoes and top pair of trousers.*)

ISABEL: Whatever you say. You couldn't come later—hey, could you? I was just ready to go to sleep, I had a long night.

JOE: I can't, I gotta catch the girls before they get to the office, they like a flower on the desk. And later I'm too tired.

ISABEL: Ain't that uncomfortable—hey? Two pairs of pants?

JOE: It's freezing cold on that subway platform. The wind's like the Gobi Desert. The only problem is when you go out to pee it takes twice as long.

ISABEL: Sellin' books too—hey?

JOE: No, I'm reading that. Trying not to forget the English language. All I hear all day is shit, fuck, and piss. I keep meaning to tell you, Isabel, it's so relaxing to talk to you, especially when you don't understand about seventy percent of what I'm saying.

ISABEL (*laughs, complimented*): Hey!

JOE (*takes her hand*): In here I feel my sanity coming back, to a certain extent. Down in the subway all day I really wonder maybe some kind of lunacy is taking over. People stand there waiting for the train, talking to themselves. And loud, with gestures. And the number of men who come up behind me and feel my ass. (*With a sudden drop in all his confidence:*) What scares me, see, is that I'm getting too nervous to pick up a drill—if I ever get to practice dentistry at all, I mean. The city . . . is crazy! A hunchback yesterday suddenly comes up to me . . . apropos of nothing . . . and he starts yelling, "You will not find one word about democracy in the Constitution, this is a Christian Republic!" Nobody laughed. The Nazi swastika is blossoming out all over the toothpaste ads. And it seems to be getting worse—there's a guy on Forty-eighth Street and Eighth Avenue selling two hotdogs for seven cents! What can he make?

ISABEL: Two for *seven*? Jesus.

JOE: I tell you I get the feeling every once in a while that some bright morning millions of people are going to come pouring out of the buildings and just . . . I don't know what . . . kill each other? Or only the Jews? Or just maybe sit down on the sidewalk and cry. (*Now he turns to her and starts to climb up on the bed beside her.*)

ISABEL (*looking at the book*): It's about families?

JOE: No, it's just called *The Origin of the Family, Private Property, and the State,* by Friedrich Engels. Marxism.

ISABEL: What's that?

JOE (*his head resting on hers, his hand holding her breast*): Well, it's the idea that all of our relationships are basically ruled by it's the idea that all of our relationships are basically ruled by money.

ISABEL (*nodding, as she well knows*): Oh, right—hey, yeah.

JOE (*raising himself up*): No, it's not what you think . . .

ISABEL: It's a whole book about *that*?

JOE: It's about socialism, where the girls would all have jobs so they wouldn't have to do this, see.

ISABEL: Oh! But what would the guys do, though?

JOE (*flustered*): Well . . . like for instance if I had money to open an office I would probably get married very soon.

ISABEL: Yeah, but I get married guys. (*Brightly:*) And I even get two dentists that you brought me . . . Bernie and Allan? . . . and they've got offices, too.

JOE: You don't understand. . . . He shows that underneath our ideals it's all economics between people, and it shouldn't be.

ISABEL: What should it be?

JOE: Well, you know, like . . . love.

ISABEL: Ohhh! Well that's nice—hey. You think I could read it?

JOE: Sure, try. . . . I'd like your reaction. I like you early, Isabel, you look so fresh. Gives me an illusion.

ISABEL: I'm sorry if I'm tired.

JOE (*kisses her, trying to rouse himself*): Say . . . did Bernie finish the filling?

ISABEL: Yeah, he polished yesterday.

JOE: Open.

She opens her mouth.

Bernie's good. (*Proudly:*) I told you, we were in the same class. Say hello when you see him again.

ISABEL: He said he might come after five. He always says to give you his best.

JOE: Give him my best, too.

ISABEL (*readying herself on the bed*): Till you I never had so many dentists.

He lowers onto her. Fadeout.

Lights come up on BANKS, *suspended in a painter's cradle, painting a bridge. He sings a verse of "Backbone and Navel Doin' the Belly Rub," then speaks.*

BANKS: Sometimes you'd get the rumor they be hirin' in New York City, so we all went to New York City, but they wasn't nothin' in New York City, so we'd head for Lima, Ohio; Detroit, Michigan; Duluth, Minnesota; or go down Baltimore; or Alabama or Decatur, Illinois. But anywhere you'd go was always a jail. I was in a chain gang in Georgia pickin' cotton for four months just for hoboin' on a train. That was 1935 in the summertime, and when they set me free they give me thirty-five cents. Yes, sir, thirty-five cents is what they give me, pickin' cotton four months against my will. (*Pause.*) Yeah, I still hear that train, that long low whistle, *whoo-ooo!*

Fadeout. Lights come up on ROSE, *seated at the piano, playing. Two moving men in work aprons enter, raise her hands from the piano, and push the piano off.*

ROSE (*half to herself, furious*): How stupid it all is. How stupid! (*Prayerfully:*) Oh, my dear Lee, wherever you are—believe in something. Anything. But believe. (*She turns and moves off with the piano stool, as though emptied out.*)

Lights come up on LEE, *sitting at an open-air café table under a tree.* ISAAC, *the black proprietor, brings him a water-melon slice.*

ISAAC: You been workin' the river long? I ain't seen you before, have I?

LEE: No, this is my first trip down the river, I'm from New York City—I'm just kind of looking around the country, talking to people.

ISAAC: What you lookin' around *for*?

LEE: Nothing—just trying to figure out what's happening. Ever hear of Mark Twain?

ISAAC: He from round here?

LEE: Well, long time ago, yeah. He was a story writer.

ISAAC: Unh-unh. I ain't seen him around here. You ask at the post office?

LEE: No, but I might. I'm kind of surprised you can get fifteen cents a slice down here these days.

ISAAC: Ohhh—white folks *loves* watermelon. Things as bad as this up North?

LEE: Probably not quite. I sure wouldn't want to be one of you people down here . . . specially with this Depression.

ISAAC: Mister, if I was to tell you the God's honest truth, the main thing about the Depression is that it finally hit the white people. 'Cause us folks never had nothin' else. (*He looks offstage.*) Well, now—here come the big man.

LEE: He trouble?

ISAAC: He's anything he wants to be, mister—he the sheriff.

The SHERIFF *enters, wearing holstered gun, boots, badge, broad-brimmed hat, and carrying something wrapped under his arm. He silently stares at* LEE, *then turns to* ISAAC.

SHERIFF: Isaac?

ISAAC: Yes, sir.

SHERIFF (*after a moment*): Sit down.

ISAAC: Yes, sir.

He sits on a counter stool; he is intensely curious about the Sheriff's calling on him but not frightened. The SHERIFF *seems to be having trouble with Lee's strange presence.*

LEE (*makes a nervous half-apology*): I'm off the boat. (*He indicates offstage.*)

SHERIFF: You don't bother me, boy—relax.

He sits and sets his package down and turns with gravity to ISAAC. LEE *makes himself unobtrusive and observes in silence.*

ISAAC: Looks like rain.

SHERIFF (*preoccupied*): Mm . . . hard to know.

ISAAC: Yeah . . . always is in Louisiana. (*Pause.*) Anything I can do for you, Sheriff?

SHERIFF: Read the papers today?

ISAAC: I couldn't read my name if an air-o-plane wrote it in the sky, Sheriff, you know that.

SHERIFF: My second cousin Allan? The state senator?

ISAAC: Uh-huh?

SHERIFF: The governor just appointed him. He's gonna help run the state police.

ISAAC: Uh-huh?

SHERIFF: He's comin' down to dinner Friday night over to my house. Bringin' his wife and two daughters. I'm gonna try to talk to Allan about a job on the state police. They still paying the *state* police, see.

ISAAC: Uh-huh. Well, that be nice, won't it.

SHERIFF: Isaac, I like you to cook me up some of that magical fried chicken around six o'clock Friday night. Okay? I'll pick it up.

ISAAC (*noncommittal*): Mm.

SHERIFF: That'd be for . . . let's see . . . (*counts on his fingers*) . . . eight people. My brother and his wife comin' over too, 'cause I aim to give Allan a little spread there, get him talkin' real good, y'know.

ISAAC: Mm.

An embarrassed pause.

SHERIFF: What's that gonna cost me for eight people, Isaac?

ISAAC (*at once*): Ten dollars.

SHERIFF: Ten.

ISAAC (*with a little commiseration*): That's right, Sheriff.

SHERIFF (*slight pause; starts to unwrap radio*): Want to show you something here, Isaac. My radio, see?

ISAAC: Uh-huh. (*He runs his hand over it.*) Play?

SHERIFF: Sure! Plays real good. I give twenty-nine ninety-five for that two years ago.

ISAAC (*looks in the back of it*): I plug it in?

SHERIFF: Go right ahead, sure. You sure painted this place up real nice. Like a real restaurant. You oughta thank the Lord, Isaac.

ISAAC (*takes out the wire and plugs it in*): I sure do. The Lord and fried chicken!

SHERIFF: You know, the county ain't paid nobody at all in three months now . . .

ISAAC: Yeah, I know. Where you switch it on?

SHERIFF: Just turn the knob. There you are. (*He turns it on.*) They're still payin' the *state* police, see. And I figure if I can get Allan to put me on—

Radio music. It is very faint.

ISAAC: Cain't hardly hear it.

SHERIFF (*angrily*): Hell, Isaac, gotta get the aerial out! (*Untangling a wire at the back of the set:*) You give me eight fried chicken dinners and I let you hold this for collateral, okay? Here we go now.

The SHERIFF backs away, stretching out the aerial wire, and Roosevelt's voice suddenly comes on strong. The SHERIFF holds still, the wire held high. LEE is absorbed.

ROOSEVELT: Clouds of suspicion, tides of ill-will and intolerance gather darkly in many places. In our own land we enjoy, indeed, a fullness of life . . .

SHERIFF: And nice fat chickens, hear? Don't give me any little old scruffy chickens.

ISAAC (*of Roosevelt*): Who's that talkin'?

ROOSEVELT: . . . greater than that of most nations. But the rush of modern civilization itself has raised for us new difficulties . . .

SHERIFF: Sound like somebody up North.

ISAAC: Hush! (*To* LEE:) Hey, that's Roosevelt, ain't it?

LEE: Yes.

ISAAC: Sure! That's the President!

SHERIFF: How about it, we got a deal? Or not?

ISAAC *has his head close to the radio, absorbed.* LEE *comes closer, bends over to listen.*

ROOSEVELT: . . . new problems which must be solved if we are to preserve to the United States the political and economic freedom for which Washington and Jefferson planned and fought. We seek not merely to make government a mechanical implement, but to give it the vibrant personal character that is the embodiment of human charity. We are poor indeed if this nation cannot afford to lift from every recess of American life the dark fear of the unemployed that they are not needed in the world. We cannot afford to accumulate a deficit in the books of human fortitude.

SIDNEY *and* DORIS *enter as lights fade on* LEE, ISAAC, *and the* SHERIFF.

SIDNEY: What's the matter? Boy, you can change quicker than . . .

DORIS (*shaking her head, closing her eyes*): I can't help it, it keeps coming back to me.

SIDNEY: How can you let a dope like Francey bother you like this?

DORIS: Because she's spreading it all over the class! And I still don't understand how you could have said a thing like that.

SIDNEY: Hon . . . all I said was that if we ever got married I would probably live downstairs. Does that mean that that's the reason we'd get married? Francey is just jealous!

DORIS (*deeply hurt*): I just wish you hadn't said that.

SIDNEY: You mean you think I'd do a thing like that for an *apartment*? What must you think of me! . . .

DORIS (*sobs*): It's just that I love you so much! . . .

SIDNEY: If I could only sell a song! Or even pass the post office exam. Then I'd have my own money, and all this garbage would stop.

DORIS: . . . I said I love you, why don't *you* say something?

SIDNEY: I love you, I love you, but I tell ya, you know what I think?

DORIS: What?

SIDNEY: Honestly—I think we ought to talk about seeing other people for a while.

DORIS (*uncomprehending*): What other people?

SIDNEY: Going out. You're still a little young, honey . . . and even at my age, it's probably not a good idea for us if we never even went out with somebody else—

DORIS: Well, who . . . do you want to take out?

SIDNEY: Nobody! . . .

DORIS: Then what do you mean?

SIDNEY: Well, it's not that I *want* to.

DORIS: Yeah, but who?

SIDNEY: Well, I don't know . . . like maybe . . . what's-her-name, Margie Ganz's sister . . .

DORIS (*alarmed*): You mean Esther Ganz with the . . . ? (*She cups her hands to indicate big breasts.*)

SIDNEY: Then *not* her!

DORIS (*hurt*): You want to take out *Esther Ganz*?

SIDNEY: I'm not saying *necessarily*! But . . . for instance, you could go out with Georgie.

DORIS: Which Georgie?

SIDNEY: Georgie Krieger.

DORIS: You're putting me with *Georgie Krieger* and *you* go out with *Esther Ganz*?

SIDNEY: It was only an *example*!

DORIS (*with incredulous distaste*): But Georgie *Krieger*! . . .

SIDNEY: Forget Georgie Krieger! Make it . . . all right, *you* pick somebody, then.

DORIS (*stares, reviewing faces*): Well . . . how about Morris?

SIDNEY (*asking the heart-stopping question*): What Morris? You mean Morris from . . .

DORIS: Yeah, Morris from the shoe store.

SIDNEY (*glimpsing quite a different side of her*): *Really?*

DORIS: Well, didn't he go a year to City College?

SIDNEY: No, he did not, he went one semester—and he *still* walks around with a comb in his pocket. . . . I think maybe we just better wait.

DORIS: I don't know, maybe it would be a good idea . . . at least till I'm a little older . . .

SIDNEY: No, we'll wait, we'll think it over.

DORIS: But you know . . .

SIDNEY (*with high anxiety*): *We'll think it over*, hon! . . .

> *He goes to the piano, plays a progression. She comes to him, then runs her fingers through his hair.*

DORIS: Play "Sittin' Around"?

SIDNEY: It's not any good.

DORIS: What do you mean, it's your greatest! Please!

SIDNEY (*sighs, sings*):
  You've got me
  Sittin' around
  Just watching shadows

On the wall;
You've got me
Sittin' around,
And all my hopes beyond recall;

I want to hear
The words of love,
I want to feel
Your lips on mine,

DORIS:
And know
The days and nights
There in your arms.

SIDNEY and DORIS:
Instead I'm . . .

Sittin' around
And all the world
Is passing by,
You've got me
Sittin' around
Like I was only
Born to cry,

When will I know
The words of love,
Your lips on mine—
Instead of

Sittin' around,
Sittin' around,
Sittin' around . . .

Fadeout. A large crowd emerges from darkness as a row of factory-type lights descend, illuminating rows of benches and scattered chairs. This is an emergency welfare office temporarily set up to handle the flood of desperate people. A

WELFARE WORKER *hands each applicant a sheet of paper and then wanders off.*

MOE: I don't understand this. I distinctly read in the paper that anybody wants to work can go direct to WPA and they fix you up with a job.

LEE: They changed it. You can only get a WPA job now if you get on relief first.

MOE (*pointing toward the line*): So this is not the WPA.

LEE: I told you, Pa, this is the relief office.

MOE: Like . . . welfare.

LEE: Look, if it embarrasses you—

MOE: Listen, if it has to be done it has to be done. Now let me go over it again—what do I say?

LEE: You refuse to let me live in the house. We don't get along.

MOE: Why can't you live at home?

LEE: If I can live at home, I don't need relief. That's the rule.

MOE: Okay. So I can't stand the sight of you.

LEE: Right.

MOE: So you live with your friend in a rooming house.

LEE: Correct.

MOE: . . . They're gonna believe that?

LEE: Why not? I've got a few clothes over there.

MOE: All this for twenty-two dollars a week?

LEE (*angering*): What am I going to do? Even old-time newspapermen are out of work. . . . See, if I can get on the WPA Writers Project, at least I'd get experience if a real job comes along. I've explained this a dozen times, Pa, there's nothing complicated.

MOE (*unsatisfied*): I'm just trying to get used to it. All right.

> *They embrace.*

We shouldn't look too friendly, huh?

LEE (*laughs*): That's the idea!

MOE: I don't like you, and you can't stand the sight of me.

LEE: That's it! (*He laughs.*)

MOE (*to the air, with mock outrage*): So he laughs.

> *They move into the crowd and find seats in front of* RYAN, *the supervisor, at a desk.*

RYAN: Matthew R. Bush!

> *A very dignified man of forty-five rises, crosses, and follows* RYAN *out.*

MOE: Looks like a butler.

LEE: Probably was.

MOE (*shakes his head mournfully*): Hmm!

ROBERTSON (*from choral area*): I did a lot of walking back in those days, and the contrasts were startling. Along the West Side of Manhattan you had eight or ten of the world's greatest ocean liners tied up—I recall the SS *Manhattan,* the *Berengaria,* the *United States*—most of them would never sail again. But at the same time they were putting up the Empire State Building, highest in the world. But with whole streets and avenues of empty stores who would ever rent space in it?

> *A baby held by* GRACE, *a young woman in the back, cries.* MOE *turns to look, then stares ahead.*

MOE: Lee, what'll you do if they give you a pick-and-shovel job?

LEE: I'll take it.

MOE: You'll dig holes in the streets?

LEE: It's no disgrace, Dad.

ROBERTSON: It was incredible to me how long it was lasting. I would never, never have believed we could not recover before this. The years were passing, a whole generation was withering in the best years of its life . . .

The people in the crowd start talking: KAPUSH, *Slavonic, in his late sixties, with a moustache;* DUGAN, *an Irishman;* IRENE, *a middle-aged black woman;* TOLAND, *a cabbie.*

KAPUSH (*with ferocious frustration*): What can you expect from a country that puts a frankfurter on the Supreme Court? Felix the Frankfurter. Look it up.

DUGAN (*from another part of the room*): Get back in the clock, ya cuckoo!

KAPUSH (*turning his body around angrily to face* DUGAN *and jarring* IRENE, *sitting next to him*): Who's talkin' to me!

IRENE: Hey, now, don't mess with me, mister!

DUGAN: Tell him, tell him!

RYAN *rushes in. He is pale, his vest is loaded with pens and pencils, and a sheaf of papers is in his hand. A tired man.*

RYAN: We gonna have another riot, folks? Is that what we're gonna have? Mr. Kapush, I told you three days running now, if you live in Bronx, you've got to apply in Bronx.

KAPUSH: It's all right, I'll wait.

RYAN (*as he passes* DUGAN): Leave him alone, will you? He's a little upset in his mind.

DUGAN: He's a fascist. I seen him down Union Square plenty of times.

IRENE *slams her walking stick down on the table.*

RYAN: Oh, Jesus . . . here we go again.

IRENE: Gettin' on to ten o'clock, Mr. Ryan.

RYAN: I've done the best I can, Irene . . .

IRENE: That's what the good Lord said when he made the jackass, but he decided to knuckle down and try harder. People been thrown out on the sidewalk, mattresses, pots and pans, and everything else they own. Right on A Hundred and Thirty-eighth Street. They goin' back in their apartments today or we goin' raise us some real hell.

RYAN: I've got no more appropriations for you till the first of the month, and that's it, Irene.

IRENE: Mr. Ryan, you ain't talkin' to me, you talkin' to Local Forty-five of the Workers Alliance, and you know what that mean.

DUGAN (*laughs*): Communist Party.

IRENE: That's right, mister, and they don't mess. So why don't you get on your phone and call Washington. And while you're at it, you can remind Mr. Roosevelt that I done swang One Hundred and Thirty-ninth Street for him in the last election, and if he want it swung again he better get crackin'!

RYAN: Holy Jesus.

He hurries away, but LEE *tries to delay him.*

LEE: I was told to bring my father.

RYAN: What?

LEE: Yesterday. You told me to—

RYAN: Get off my back, will ya? (*He hurries out.*)

DUGAN: This country's gonna end up on the top of the trees throwin' coconuts at each other.

MOE (*quietly to* LEE): I hope I can get out by eleven, I got an appointment with a buyer.

TOLAND (*next to* MOE, *with a* Daily News *open in his hands*): Boy, oh, boy, looka this—Helen Hayes gonna put on forty pounds to play Victoria Regina.

MOE: Who's that?

TOLAND: Queen of England.

MOE: She was so fat?

TOLAND: Victoria? Horse. I picked up Helen Hayes when I had my cab. Very small girl. And Adolphe Menjou once—he was small too. I even had Al Smith once, way back before he was governor. He was real small.

MOE: Maybe your cab was large.

TOLAND: What do you mean? I had a regular Ford.

MOE: You lost it?

TOLAND: What're you gonna do? The town is walkin'. I paid five hundred dollars for a new Ford, including bumpers and a spare. But thank God, at least I got into the housing project. It's nice and reasonable.

MOE: What do you pay?

TOLAND: Nineteen fifty a month. It sounds like a lot, but we got three nice rooms—providin' I get a little help here. What's your line?

MOE: I sell on commission right now. I used to have my own business.

TOLAND: Used-ta. Whoever you talk to, "I used-ta." If they don't do something, I tell ya, one of these days this used-ta be a country.

KAPUSH (*exploding*): Ignorance, ignorance! People don't know facts. Greatest public library system in the entire world and nobody goes in but Jews.

MOE (*glancing at him*): Ah-ha.

LEE: What're you, Iroquois?

DUGAN: He's a fascist. I seen him talking on Union Square.

IRENE: Solidarity, folks, black and white together, that's what we gotta have. Join the Workers Alliance, ten cents a month, and you git yourself some solidarity.

KAPUSH: I challenge anybody to find the word democracy in the Constitution. This is a republic! *Demos* is the Greek word for mob.

DUGAN (*imitating the bird*): *Cuckoo!*

KAPUSH: Come to get my money and the bank is closed up! Four thousand dollars up the flue. Thirteen years in hardware, savin' by the week.

DUGAN: Mental diarrhea.

KAPUSH: Mobocracy. Gimme, gimme, gimme, all they know.

DUGAN: So what're *you* doing here?

KAPUSH: Roosevelt was sworn in on a Dutch Bible! (*Silence.*) Anybody know that? (*To* IRENE:) Betcha didn't know that, did you?

IRENE: You givin' me a headache, mister . . .

KAPUSH: I got nothin' against colored. Colored never took my store away. Here's my bankbook, see that? Bank of the United States. See that? Four thousand six hundred and ten dollars and thirty-one cents, right? Who's got that money? Savin' thirteen years, by the week. *Who's got my money?*

> He has risen to his feet. His fury has turned the moment silent. MATTHEW BUSH *enters and sways.* RYAN *enters.*

RYAN (*calls*): Arthur Clayton!

CLAYTON (*starts toward* RYAN *from the crowd and indicates* BUSH):
I think there's something the matter with—

> BUSH *collapses on the floor. For a moment no one moves. Then*
> IRENE *goes to him, bends over him.*

IRENE: Hey. Hey, mister.

> LEE *helps him up and sits him in the chair.*

RYAN (*calling*): Myrna, call the ambulance!

> IRENE *lightly slaps Bush's cheeks.*

LEE: You all right?

RYAN (*looking around*): Clayton?

CLAYTON: I'm Clayton.

RYAN (*Clayton's form in his hand*): You're not eligible for relief;
you've got furniture and valuables, don't you?

CLAYTON: But nothing I could realize anything on.

RYAN: Why not?

IRENE: This man's starvin', Mr. Ryan.

RYAN: What're you, a medical doctor now, Irene? I called the
ambulance! Now don't start makin' an issue, will you? (*To*
CLAYTON:) Is this your address? Gramercy Park South?

CLAYTON (*embarrassed*): That doesn't mean a thing. I haven't
really eaten in a few days, actually . . .

RYAN: Where do you get that kind of rent?

CLAYTON: I haven't paid my rent in over eight months . . .

RYAN (*starting away*): Forget it, mister, you got valuables and
furniture; you can't—

CLAYTON: I'm very good at figures, I was in brokerage. I thought if I could get anything that required . . . say statistics . . .

IRENE: Grace? You got anything in that bottle?

> GRACE, *in a rear row with a baby in her arms, reaches forward with a baby bottle that has an inch of milk at the bottom. She hands the bottle to* IRENE.

GRACE: Ain't much left there . . .

IRENE (*takes nipple off bottle*): Okay, now, open your mouth, mister.

> BUSH *gulps the milk.*

There, look at that, see? Man's starvin'!

MOE (*stands, reaching into his pocket*): Here . . . look . . . for God's sake. (*He takes out change and picks out a dime.*) Why don't you send down, get him a bottle of milk?

IRENE (*calls toward a young woman in the back*): Lucy?

LUCY (*coming forward*): Here I am, Irene.

IRENE: Go down the corner, bring a bottle of milk.

> MOE *gives her the dime, and* LUCY *hurries out.*

And a couple of straws, honey! You in bad shape, mister—why'd you wait so long to get on relief?

BUSH: Well . . . I just don't like the idea, you know.

IRENE: Yeah, I know—you a real bourgeoisie. Let me tell you something—

BUSH: I'm a chemist.

IRENE: I believe it, too—you so educated you sooner die than say brother. Now lemme tell you people. (*Addressing the crowd:*) Time has come to say brother. My husband pass away and leave me with three small children. No money, no work—I's about ready to stick my head in the cookin' stove. Then the city marshal come and take my chest of drawers, bed, and table, and leave me sittin' on a old orange crate in the middle of the room. And it come over me, mister, come over me to get mean. And I got real mean. Go down in the street and start yellin' and howlin' like a real mean woman. And the people crowd around the marshal truck, and 'fore you know it that marshal turn himself around and go on back downtown empty-handed. And that's when I see it. I see the solidarity, and I start to preach it up and down. 'Cause I got me a stick, and when I start poundin' time with this stick, a whole lot of people starts to march, keepin' time. We shall not be moved, yeah, we shall in no wise be disturbed. Some days I goes to court with my briefcase, raise hell with the judges. Ever time I goes into court the cops commence to holler, "Here comes that old lawyer woman!" But all I got in here is some old newspaper and a bag of cayenne pepper. Case any cop start musclin' me around—that hot pepper, that's hot cayenne pepper. And if the judge happen to be Catholic I got my rosary layin' in there, and I kind of let that crucifix hang out so's they think I'm Catholic too. (*She draws a rosary out of her bag and lets it hang over the side.*)

LUCY (*enters with milk*): Irene!

IRENE: Give it here, Lucy. Now drink it slow, mister. Slow, slow . . .

> BUSH *is drinking in sips. People now go back into themselves, read papers, stare ahead.*

RYAN: Lee Baum!

LEE (*hurries to* MOE): Here! Okay, Dad, let's go.

> LEE *and* MOE *go to Ryan's desk.*

RYAN: This your father?

MOE: Yes.

RYAN (*to* MOE): Where's he living now?

LEE: I don't live at home because—

RYAN: Let *him* answer. Where's he living, Mr. Baum?

MOE: Well, he . . . he rents a room someplace.

RYAN: You gonna sit there and tell me you won't let him in the house?

MOE (*with great difficulty*): I won't let him in, no.

RYAN: You mean you're the kind of man, if he rang the bell and you opened the door and saw him, you wouldn't let him inside?

MOE: Well, naturally, if he just wants to come in the house—

LEE: I don't want to live there—

RYAN: I don't care what *you* want, fella. (*To* MOE:) You will let him into the house, right?

MOE (*stiffening*): . . . I can't stand the sight of him.

RYAN: Why? I saw you both sitting here talking together the last two hours.

MOE: We weren't talking. . . . We were arguing, fighting! . . .

RYAN: Fighting about what?

MOE (*despite himself, growing indignant*): Who can remember? We were fighting, we're always fighting! . . .

RYAN: Look, Mr. Baum . . . you're employed, aren't you?

MOE: I'm employed? Sure I'm employed. Here. (*He holds up the folded* Times.) See? Read it yourself. R. H. Macy, right? Ladies' full-length slip, genuine Japanese silk, hand-embroidered with lace top and trimmings, two ninety-eight. My boss makes four cents on these, I make a tenth of a cent. That's how I'm employed!

RYAN: You'll let him in the house. (*He starts to move.*)

MOE: I will not let him in the house! He . . . he don't believe in anything!

> LEE *and* RYAN *look at* MOE *in surprise.* MOE *himself is caught off balance by his genuine outburst and rushes out.* RYAN *glances at* LEE, *stamps a requisition form, and hands it to him, convinced.* RYAN *exits.*
>
> LEE *moves slowly, staring at the form. The welfare clients exit, the row of overhead lights flies out.*
>
> *Lights come up on* ROBERTSON.

ROBERTSON: Then and now, you have to wonder what really held it all together, and maybe it was simply the Future: the people were still not ready to give it up. Like a God, it was always worshiped among us, and they could not yet turn their backs on it. Maybe it's that simple. Because from any objective viewpoint, I don't understand why it held.

> *The people from the relief office form a line as on a subway platform.* JOE *comes behind the line singing and offering flowers from a basket. There is the sound of an approaching train, its windows flashing light.* JOE *throws himself under it: a squeal of brakes. The crowd sings "In New York City, You Really Got to Know Your Line," one by one taking the lyrics, ending in a chorus. Fadeout.*
>
> *Lights come up on* EDIE. LEE *is in spotlight.*

LEE (*to audience*): Any girl with an apartment of her own was beautiful. She was one of the dialogue writers for the *Superman* comic strip. (*To her:*) Edie, can I sleep here tonight?

EDIE: Oh, hi, Lee—yeah, sure. Let me finish and I'll put a sheet on the couch. If you have any laundry, throw it in the sink. I'm going to wash later.

> *He stands behind her as she works.*

This is going to be a terrific sequence.

LEE: It's amazing to me how you can keep your mind on it.

EDIE: He's also a great teacher of class consciousness.

LEE: Superman?

EDIE: He stands for justice!

LEE: Oh! You mean under capitalism you can't . . .

EDIE: Sure! The implications are terrific. (*She works lovingly for a moment.*)

LEE: Y'know, you're beautiful when you talk about politics, your face lights up.

EDIE (*smiling*): Don't be such a bourgeois horse's ass. I'll get your sheet. (*She starts up.*)

LEE: Could I sleep in your bed tonight? I don't know what it is lately—I'm always lonely. Are you?

EDIE: Sometimes. But a person doesn't have to go to bed with people to be connected to mankind.

LEE: You're right. I'm ashamed of myself.

EDIE: Why don't you join the Party?

LEE: I guess I don't want to ruin my chances; I want to be a sportswriter.

EDIE: You could write for the *Worker* sports page.

LEE: The *Daily Worker* sports page?

EDIE: Then help improve it! Why are you so defeatist, hundreds of people are joining the Party every week.

LEE: I don't know why, maybe I'm too skeptical—or cynical. Like . . . when I was in Flint, Michigan, during the sit-down strike. Thought I'd write a feature story . . . all those thousands of men barricaded in the GM plant, the wives hoisting food up to the windows in baskets. It was like the French Revolution. But then I got to talk to them as individuals, and the prejudice! The ignorance! . . . In the Ford plant there was damn near a race war because some of the Negro workers didn't want to join the strike. . . . It was murderous.

EDIE: Well, they're still backward, I know that.

LEE: No, they're normal. I really wonder if there's going to be time to save this country from itself. You ever wonder that? You do, don't you.

EDIE (*fighting the temptation to give way*): You really want my answer?

LEE: Yes.

EDIE: We're picketing the Italian consulate tomorrow, to protest Mussolini sending Italian troops to the Spanish Civil War. Come! *Do* something! You love Hemingway so much, read what he just said—"One man alone is no fucking good." As decadent as he is, even *he's* learning.

LEE: Really, your face gets so beautiful when you . . .

EDIE: Anyone can be beautiful if what they believe is beautiful! I believe in my comrades. I believe in the Soviet Union. I believe in the working class and the peace of the whole world when socialism comes . . .

LEE: Boy, you really are wonderful. Look, now that I'm on relief can I take you out to dinner? I'll pay, I mean.

EDIE (*smiles*): Why must you pay for me, just because I'm a woman?

LEE: Right! I forgot about that.

EDIE (*working*): I've got to finish this panel. . . . I'll make up the couch in a minute. . . . What about the Writer's Project, you getting on?

LEE: I think so; they're putting people on to write a WPA Guide, it's going to be a detailed history of every section of the country. I might get sent up to the Lake Champlain district. Imagine? They're interviewing direct descendants of the soldiers who fought the Battle of Fort Ticonderoga. Ethan Allen and the Green Mountain Boys?

EDIE: Oh, yes! They beat the British up there.

LEE: It's a wonderful project; 'cause people really don't know their own history.

EDIE (*with longing and certainty*): When there's socialism everyone will.

LEE (*leaning over to look at her work*): Why don't you have Superman get laid? Or married even.

EDIE: He's much too busy.

> *He comes closer to kiss her; she starts to respond, then rejects.*

What are you *doing*?

LEE: When you say the word "socialism" your face gets so beautiful . . .

EDIE: You're totally cynical, aren't you.

LEE: Why!

EDIE: You pretend to have a serious conversation when all you want is to jump into my bed; it's the same attitude you have to the auto workers . . .

LEE: I can't see the connection between the auto workers and . . . !

EDIE (*once again on firm ground*): Everything is connected! I have to ask you to leave!

LEE: Edie!

EDIE: You are not a good person! (*She bursts into tears and rushes off.*)

LEE (*alone, full of remorse*): She's right, too! (*He exits.*)

> GRANDPA *enters from choral area, sits with his newspaper, and is immediately immersed. Then Rose's niece* LUCILLE, *her sister* FANNY, *and* DORIS, *who wears a bathrobe, carry folding chairs and seat themselves around a table.* LUCILLE *deals cards. Now* ROSE *begins speaking within the choral area, and as she speaks, she moves onto the stage proper.*

ROSE: That endless Brooklyn July! That little wooden house baking in the heat. (*She enters the stage.*) I never smelled an owl, but in July the smell of that attic crept down the stairs, and to me it smelled as dry and dusty as an owl. (*She surveys the women staring at their cards.*) From Coney Island to Brooklyn Bridge, how many thousands of women waited out the afternoons dreaming at their cards and praying for luck? Ah, luck, luck . . .

DORIS: Sidney's finishing a beautiful new song, Aunt Rose.

ROSE (*sitting at the table, taking up her hand of cards*): Maybe this one'll be lucky for you. Why are you always in a bathrobe?

DORIS: I'm only half a block away.

ROSE: But you're so young! Why don't you get dressed and leave the block once in a while?

FANNY (*smugly*): All my girls love it home, too.

ROSE: It's you, isn't it?

FANNY (*brushing dandruff off her bosom and nervously examining her cards*): I'm trying to make up my mind.

ROSE: Concentrate. Forget your dandruff for a minute.

FANNY: It wasn't dandruff, it was a thread.

ROSE: Her dandruff is threads. It's an obsession.

LUCILLE: I didn't tell you; this spring she actually called me and my sisters to come and spend the day cleaning her house.

FANNY: What's so terrible! We used to have the most marvelous times the four of us cleaning the house . . . (*Suddenly:*) It's turning into an oven in here.

LUCILLE: I'm going to faint.

ROSE: Don't faint, all the windows are open in the back of the house. We're supposed to be away.

FANNY: But there's no draft. . . . For Papa's sake . . .

LUCILLE: Why couldn't you be away and you left a window open? . . . Just don't answer the door.

ROSE: I don't want to take the chance. This one is a professional collector, I've seen him do it; if a window's open he tries to listen. They're merciless. . . . I sent Stanislaus for lemons, we'll have cold lemonade. Play.

FANNY: I can't believe they'd actually evict you, Rose.

ROSE: You can't? Wake up, Fanny. It's a bank—may they choke after the fortune of money we kept in there all those years! Ask them for two hundred dollars now and they . . . (*Tears start to her eyes.*)

FANNY: Rose, dear, come on—something'll happen, you'll see. Moe's got to find something soon, a man so well known.

LUCILLE: Couldn't he ask his mother for a little?

ROSE: His mother says there's a Depression going on. Meantime you can go blind from the diamonds on her fingers. Which he gave her! The rottenness of people! I tell you, the next time I start believing in anybody or anything I hope my tongue is cut out!

DORIS: Maybe Lee should come back and help out?

ROSE: Never! Lee is going to think his own thoughts and face the facts. He's got nothing to learn from us. Let him help himself.

LUCILLE: But to take up Communism—

ROSE: Lucille, what do you know about it? What does anybody know about it? The newspapers? The newspapers said the stock market will never come down again.

LUCILLE: But they're against God, Aunt Rose.

ROSE: I'm overjoyed you got so religious, Lucille, but please for God's sake don't tell me about it again!

FANNY (*rises, starts to leave*): I'll be right down.

ROSE: Now she's going to pee on her finger for luck.

FANNY: All right! So I won't go! (*She returns to her chair.*) And I wasn't going to pee on my finger!

ROSE: So what're we playing—cards or statues?

DORIS *sits looking at her cards, full of confusion.*

GRANDPA (*putting down his paper*): Why do they need this election?

ROSE: What do you mean, why they need this election?

GRANDPA: But everybody knows Roosevelt is going to win again. I still think he's too radical, but to go through another election is a terrible waste of money.

ROSE: What are you talking about, Papa—it's four years, they have to have an election.

GRANDPA: Why! If they decided to make him king . . .

ROSE: King!

FANNY (*pointing at* GRANDPA, *agreeing and laughing*): Believe me!

GRANDPA: If he was king he wouldn't have to waste all his time making these ridiculous election speeches, and maybe he could start to improve things!

ROSE: If I had a stamp I'd write him a letter.

GRANDPA: He could be another Kaiser Franz Joseph. Then after he dies you can have all the elections you want.

ROSE (*to* DORIS): Are you playing cards or hatching an egg?

DORIS (*startled*): Oh, it's my turn? (*She turns a card.*) All right; here!

ROSE: Hallelujah.

> *She plays a card. It is* LUCILLE'*s turn; she plays.*

Did you lose weight?

LUCILLE: I've been trying. I'm thinking of going back to the carnival.

> DORIS *quickly throws an anxious look toward* GRANDPA, *who is oblivious, reading.*

FANNY (*indicating* GRANDPA *secretively*): You better not mention . . .

LUCILLE: He doesn't have to know, and anyway I would never dance anymore; I'd only assist the magician and tell a few jokes. They're talking about starting up again in Jersey.

ROSE: Herby can't find anything?

LUCILLE: He's going out of his mind, Aunt Rose.

ROSE: God Almighty. So what's it going to be, Fanny?

FANNY (*feeling rushed, studying her cards*): One second! Just let me figure it out.

ROSE: When they passed around the brains this family was out to lunch.

FANNY: It's so hot in here I can't think!

ROSE: Play! I can't open the window. I'm not going to face that man again. He has merciless eyes.

> STANISLAUS, *a middle-aged seaman in T-shirt and dungarees, enters through the front door.*

You come in the front door? The mortgage man could come today!

STANISLAUS: I forgot! I didn't see anybody on the strcct, though. (*He lifts bag of lemons.*) Fresh lemonade coming up on deck. I starched all the napkins. (*He exits.*)

ROSE: Starched all the napkins . . . they're cracking like matzos. I feel like doing a fortune. (*She takes out another deck of cards, lays out a fortune.*)

LUCILLE: I don't know, Aunt Rose, is it so smart to let this man live with you?

DORIS: I would never dare! How can you sleep at night with a strange man in the cellar?

FANNY: Nooo! Stanislaus is a gentleman. (*To* ROSE:) I think he's a little bit a fairy, isn't he?

ROSE: I hope!

> *They all laugh.*

For God's sake, Fanny, play the queen of clubs!

FANNY: How did you know I had the queen of clubs!

ROSE: Because I'm smart, I voted for Herbert Hoover. I see what's been played, dear, so I figure what's left.

FANNY (*to* GRANDPA, *who continues reading*): She's a marvel, she's got Grandma's head.

ROSE: Huh! Look at this fortune.

FANNY: Here, I'm playing. (*She plays a card.*)

ROSE (*continuing to lay out the fortune*): I always feed the vagrants on the porch, but Stanislaus, when I hand him a plate of soup he says he wants to wash the windows before he eats. *Before!* That I never heard. I nearly fell over. Go ahead, Doris, it's you.

DORIS (*desperately trying to be quick*): I know just what to do, wait a minute.

> *The women freeze, study their cards; ROSE now faces front. She is quickly isolated in light.*

ROSE: When I went to school we had to sit like soldiers, with backs straight and our hands clasped on the desk; things were supposed to be upright. When the navy came up the Hudson River, you cried it was so beautiful. You even cried when they shot the Czar of Russia. He was also beautiful. President Warren Gamaliel Harding, another beauty. Mayor James J. Walker smiled like an angel, what a nose, and those tiny feet. Richard Whitney, president of the Stock Exchange, a handsome, upright man. I could name a hundred from the rotogravure! Who could know that these upright handsome men would either turn out to be crooks who would land in jail or ignoramuses? What is left to believe? The bathroom. I lock myself in and hold on to the faucets so I shouldn't scream. At my husband, my mother-in-law, at God knows what until they take me away . . . (*Returning to the fortune, and with deep anxiety:*) What the hell did I lay out here? What is this?

> *Light returns to normal.*

DORIS: "Gray's Elegy in a Country Churchyard."

ROSE: What?

FANNY (*touching her arm worriedly*): Why don't you lie down, Rose? . . .

ROSE: Lie down? . . . Why? (*To DORIS:*) What Gray's "Elegy"? What are you . . .

STANISLAUS enters rapidly, wearing a waist-length white starched waiter's jacket, a tray expertly on his shoulder, with glasses and rolled napkins. ROSE shows alarm as she lays a card down on the fortune.

STANISLAUS: It's a braw bricht moonlicht nicht tonicht—that's Scotch.

FANNY: How does he get those napkins to stand up!

ROSE (*under terrific tension, tears her gaze from the cards she laid out*): What's the jacket suddenly?

The women watch her tensely.

STANISLAUS (*saluting*): SS *Manhattan.* Captain's steward at your service.

ROSE: Will you stop this nightmare? Take the jacket off. What're you talking about, captain's steward? Who are you?

STANISLAUS: I was captain's personal steward, but they're not sailing the *Manhattan* anymore. Served J. Pierpont Morgan, John D. Rockefeller, Enrico Caruso, lousy tipper, Lionel—

ROSE (*very suspiciously*): Bring in the cookies, please.

He picks up the pitcher to pour the lemonade.

Thank you, I'll pour it. Go, please.

She doesn't look at him; he goes out. In the silence she picks up the pitcher, tilts it, but her hand is shaking, and FANNY takes the pitcher.

FANNY: Rose, dear, come upstairs . . .

ROSE: How does he look to you?

FANNY: Why? He looks very nice.

LUCILLE: He certainly keeps the house beautiful, Aunt Rose, it's like a ship.

ROSE: He's a liar, though; anything comes into his head, he says; what am I believing him for? What the hell got into me? You can tell he's full of shit, and he comes to the door, a perfect stranger, and I let him sleep in the cellar!

LUCILLE: *Shhh!*

    STANISLAUS *enters with a plate of cookies, in T-shirt again, determinedly.*

ROSE: Listen, Stanislaus . . . (*She stands.*)

STANISLAUS (*senses his imminent dismissal*): I go down to the ship chandler store tomorrow, get some special white paint, paint the whole outside the house. I got plenty of credit, don't cost you.

ROSE: I thought it over, you understand?

STANISLAUS (*with a desperate smile*): I borrow big ladder from the hardware store. And I gonna make nice curtains for the cellar windows. Taste the lemonade, I learn that in Spanish submarine. Excuse me, gotta clean out the icebox. (*He gets himself out.*)

FANNY: I think he's very sweet, Rose. . . . Here . . . (*She offers a glass of lemonade.*)

LUCILLE: Don't worry about that mortgage man, Aunt Rose, it's after five, they don't come after five . . .

ROSE (*caught in her uncertainty*): He seems sweet to you?

GRANDPA (*putting the paper down*): What Lee ought to do . . . Rosie?

ROSE: Hah?

GRANDPA: Lee should go to Russia.

    The sisters and LUCILLE *turn to him in surprise.*

ROSE (*incredulous, frightened*): To Russia?

GRANDPA: In Russia they need everything; whereas here, y'see, they don't need anything, so therefore, there's no work.

ROSE (*with an edge of hysteria*): Five minutes ago Roosevelt is too radical, and now you're sending Lee to Russia?

GRANDPA: That's different. Look what it says here . . . a hundred thousand American people applying for jobs in Russia. Look, it says it. So if Lee would go over there and open up a nice chain of clothing stores—

ROSE: Papa! You're such a big anti-Communist . . . and you don't know the government owns everything in Russia?

GRANDPA: Yeah, but not the *stores.*

ROSE: Of course the stores!

GRANDPA: The *stores* they own?

ROSE: Yes!

GRANDPA: Them bastards.

ROSE (*to* LUCILLE): I'll go out of my mind here . . .

DORIS: So who wrote it?

ROSE: Wrote what?

DORIS: "Gray's Elegy in a Country Churchyard." It was a fifteen-dollar question on the radio yesterday, but you were out. I ran to call you.

ROSE (*suppressing a scream*): Who wrote Gray's "Elegy in a Country Churchyard"?

DORIS: By the time I got back to the radio it was another question.

ROSE: Doris, darling . . . (*Slowly:*) Gray's "Elegy in a—

　　FANNY *laughs.*

　　What are you laughing at, do you know?

FANNY (*pleasantly*): How would I know?

LUCILLE: Is it Gray?

> ROSE *looks at her, an enormous sadness in her eyes. With a certain timidity,* LUCILLE *goes on:*

Well, it says "Gray's Elegy," right?

DORIS: How could it be Gray? That's the title!

> ROSE *is staring ahead in an agony of despair.*

FANNY: What's the matter, Rose?

DORIS: Well, what'd I say?

FANNY: Rose, what's the matter?

LUCILLE: You all right?

FANNY (*really alarmed, turning Rose's face to her*): What is the matter!

> ROSE *bursts into tears.* FANNY *gets up and embraces her, almost crying herself.*

Oh, Rosie, please . . . don't. It'll get better, something's got to happen . . .

> *A sound from the front door galvanizes them. A man calls from off: "Hello?"*

DORIS (*pointing*): There's some—

ROSE (*her hands flying up in fury*): Sssh! (*Whispering:*) I'll go upstairs. I'm not home.

> *She starts to go;* MOE *enters.*

DORIS (*laughing*): It's Uncle Moe!

MOE: What's the excitement?

ROSE (*going to him*): Oh, thank God, I thought it was the mortgage man. You're home early.

He stands watching her.

FANNY: Let's go, come on.

They begin to clear table of tray, lemonade, glasses, etc.

MOE (*looking into Rose's face*): You crying?

LUCILLE: How's it in the city?

ROSE: Go out the back, huh?

MOE: The city is murder.

FANNY: Will you get your bills together? I'm going downtown tomorrow. I'll save you the postage.

ROSE: Take a shower. Why are you so pale?

LUCILLE: Bye-bye, Uncle Moe.

MOE: Bye, girls.

DORIS (*as she exits with* FANNY *and* LUCILLE): I must ask him how he made that lemonade . . .

They are gone, MOE *is staring at some vision, quite calm, but absorbed.*

ROSE: You . . . sell anything? . . . No, heh?

He shakes his head negatively—but that is not what he is thinking about.

Here . . . (*She gets a glass from the table.*) Come drink, it's cold.

He takes it but doesn't drink.

MOE: You're hysterical every night.

ROSE: No, I'm all right. It's just all so stupid, and every once in a while I can't . . . I can't . . . (*She is holding her head.*)

MOE: The thing is . . . You listening to me?

ROSE: What? (*Suddenly aware of her father's pressure on* MOE, *she turns and goes quickly to him.*) Go on the back porch, Papa, huh? It's shady there now . . . (*She hands him a glass of lemonade.*)

GRANDPA: But the man'll see me.

ROSE: It's all right, he won't come so late, and Moe is here. Go . . .

> GRANDPA *starts to go.*

. . . and why don't you put on your other glasses, they're much cooler.

> GRANDPA *is gone. She returns to* MOE.

Yes, dear. What. What's going to be?

MOE: We are going to be all right.

ROSE: Why?

MOE: Because we are. So this nervousness every night is unnecessary, and I wish to God—

ROSE (*indicating the table and the cards spread out*): It's just a fortune. I . . . I started to do a fortune, and I saw . . . a young man. The death of a young man.

MOE (*struck*): You don't say.

ROSE (*sensing*): Why?

> *He turns front, amazed, frightened.*

Why'd you say that?

MOE: Nothing . . .

ROSE: Is Lee . . .

MOE: Will you cut that out—

ROSE: Tell me!

MOE: I saw a terrible thing on the subway. Somebody jumped in front of a train.

ROSE: Aaaahhh—again! My God! You saw him?

MOE: No, a few minutes before I got there. Seems he was a very young man. One of the policemen was holding a great big basket of flowers. Seems he was trying to sell flowers.

ROSE: I saw it! (*Her spine tingling, she points down at the cards.*) Look, it's there! That's death! I'm going to write Lee to come home immediately. I want you to put in that you want him home.

MOE: I have nothing for him, Rose; how can I make him come home?

ROSE (*screaming and weeping*): Then go to your mother and stand up like a man to her . . . instead of this goddamned fool! (*She weeps.*)

MOE (*stung, nearly beaten, not facing her*): This can't . . . it can't go on forever, Rose, a country can't just die!

She goes on weeping; he cries out in pain.

Will you stop? I'm trying! God Almighty, I am trying!

The doorbell rings. They start with shock. GRANDPA *enters, hurrying, pointing.*

GRANDPA: Rose—

ROSE: *Ssssh!*

The bell rings again. MOE *presses stiffened fingers against his temple, his eyes averted in humiliation.* ROSE *whispers:*

God in heaven . . . make him go away!

The bell rings again. MOE's *head is bent, his hand quivering as it grips his forehead.*

Oh, dear God, give our new President the strength, and the wisdom . . .

Door knock, a little more insistent.

... give Mr. Roosevelt the way to help us ...

Door knock.

Oh, my God, help our dear country ... and the people! ...

Door knock. Fadeout.

Lights come up on company as the distant sound of a fight crowd is heard and a clanging bell signals the end of a round. SIDNEY *enters in a guard's uniform; he is watching* LEE, *who enters smoking a cigar stub, wearing a raincoat, finishing some notes on a pad, his hat tipped back on his head.*

SIDNEY: Good fight tonight, Mr. Baum.

LEE: (*hardly glancing at him*): Huh? Yeah, pretty good.

SIDNEY *looks on, amused, as* LEE *slowly passes before him, scribbling away.*

As BANKS *speaks,* SOLDIERS *appear and repeat italicized words after him.*

BANKS: When the *war* came I was so *glad* when I got in the *army.* A man could be *killed* anytime at all on those trains, but with that uniform on I said, "Now I am safe."

SIDNEY: Hey!

LEE: Huh? (*Now he recognizes* SIDNEY.) Sidney!

SIDNEY: Boy, you're some cousin. I'm looking straight at you and no recognito! I'm chief of security here.

BANKS: I felt proud to salute and look around and see all the *good soldiers* of the United States. I was a good *soldier too*, and got five battle stars.

Other SOLDIERS *repeat, "Five, five, five."*

LEE: You still on the block?

SIDNEY: Sure. Say, you know who'd have loved to have seen you again? Lou Charney.

LEE: Charney?

RALPH: Hundred yard dash—you and him used to trot to school together . . .

LEE: Oh, Lou, sure! How is he!

SIDNEY: He's dead. Got it in Italy.

BANKS: Yeah, I seen all kinds of war—including the kind they calls . . .

COMPANY: . . . peace.

Four soldiers sing the beginning of "We're in the Money."

SIDNEY: And you knew Georgie Rosen got killed, didn't you?

LEE: Georgie Rosen.

RALPH: Little Georgie.

SIDNEY: Sold you his racing bike.

RALPH: That got stolen.

LEE: Yes, yes! God—Georgie too.

COMPANY (*whispering*): Korea.

RALPH: Lot of wars on that block.

One actor sings the first verse of "The Times They Are A'Changing."

SIDNEY: Oh, yeah—Lou Charney's kid was in *Vietnam*.

The company says "Vietnam" with SIDNEY.

Still and all, it's a great country, huh?

LEE: Why do you say that?

SIDNEY: Well, all the crime and divorce and whatnot. But one thing about people like us, you live through the worst, you know the difference between bad and *bad*.

BANKS: One time I was hoboin' through that high country—the Dakotas, Montana—I come to the monument for General Custer's last stand, Little Big Horn. And I wrote my name on it, yes, sir. For the memories; just for the note; so my name will be up there forever. Yes, sir . . .

SIDNEY: But I look back at it all now, and I don't know about you, but it seems it was friendlier. Am I right?

LEE: I'm not sure it was friendlier. Maybe people just cared more.

SIDNEY (*with* IRENE *singing "I Want to Be Happy" under his speech*): Like the songs, I mean—you listen to a thirties song, and most of them are so happy, and still—you could cry.

BANKS: But I still hear that train sometimes; still hear that long low whistle. Yes, sir, I still hear that train . . . *whoo-ooo!*

LEE: You still writing songs?

SIDNEY: Sure! I had a couple published.

RALPH: Still waiting for the big break?

SIDNEY: I got a new one now, though—love you to hear it. I'm calling it "A Moon of My Own." I don't know what happened, I'm sitting on the back porch and suddenly it came to me—"A Moon of My Own." I ran in and told Doris, she could hardly sleep all night.

> DORIS *quietly sings under the following speeches:* ". . . *and know the days and nights there in your arms. Instead I'm sittin' around . . ."*

LEE: How's Doris, are you still . . .

SIDNEY: Oh, very much so. In fact, we were just saying we're practically the only ones we know didn't get divorced.

LEE: Did I hear your mother died?

SIDNEY: Yep, Fanny's gone. I was sorry to hear about Aunt Rose, and Moe.

LEE (*over "Life Is Just a Bowl of Cherries" music*): After all these years I still can't settle with myself about my mother. In her own crazy way she was so much like the country.

> ROSE *sings the first line of "Life Is Just a Bowl of Cherries."*
> *Through the rest of Lee's speech, she sings the next four lines.*

There was nothing she believed that she didn't also believe the opposite. (ROSE *sings*.) She'd sit down on the subway next to a black man (ROSE *sings*) and in a couple of minutes she had him asking her advice (ROSE *sings*) about the most intimate things in his life. (ROSE *sings*.) Then, maybe a day later—

LEE and ROSE: "Did you hear! They say the colored are moving in!"

LEE: Or she'd lament her fate as a woman—

ROSE and LEE: "I was born twenty years too soon!"

ROSE: They treat a woman like a cow, fill her up with a baby and lock her in for the rest of her life.

LEE: But then she'd warn me, "Watch out for women—when they're not stupid, they're full of deceit." I'd come home and give her a real bath of radical idealism, and she was ready to storm the barricades; by evening she'd fallen in love again with the Prince of Wales. She was so like the country; money obsessed her, but what she really longed for was some kind of height where she could stand and see out and around and breathe in the air of her own free life. With all her defeats she believed to the end that the world was meant to be better. . . . I don't know; all I know for sure is that whenever I think of her, I always end up—with this headful of life!

ROSE (*calls, in a ghostly, remote way*): Sing!

> *Alternating lines,* LEE *and* ROSE *sing "Life Is Just a Bowl of Cherries." The whole company takes up the song in a soft, long-lost tonality.* ROBERTSON *moves forward, the music continuing underneath.*

ROBERTSON: There were moments when the word "revolution" was not rhetorical.

> TED QUINN *steps forward.*

QUINN: Roosevelt saved them; came up at the right minute and pulled the miracle.

ROBERTSON: Up to a point; but what really got us out of it was the war.

QUINN: Roosevelt gave them back their belief in the country. The government belonged to them again!

ROBERTSON: Well, I'll give you that.

QUINN: Of course you will, you're not a damned fool. The return of that belief is what saved the United States, no more, no less!

ROBERTSON: I think that's putting it a little too . . .

QUINN (*cutting him off and throwing up his hands*): That's it! . . . God, how I love that music!

> *He breaks into his soft-shoe dance as the singing grows louder. He gestures for the audience to join in, and the company does so as well as the chorus swells . . .*

END